I0004332

net results

net results

Guy Stanley and Dian Cohen

Authors Choice Press
San Jose New York Lincoln Shanghai

net results

All Rights Reserved © 2001 by Dian Cohen Productions Ltd.

No part of this book may be reproduced or transmitted in any form or by any means, graphic, electronic, or mechanical, including photocopying, recording, taping, or by any information storage or retrieval system, without the permission in writing from the publisher.

Authors Choice Press
an imprint of iUniverse.com, Inc.

For information address:
iUniverse.com, Inc.
5220 S 16th, Ste. 200
Lincoln, NE 68512
www.iuniverse.com

ISBN: 0-595-19087-1

Printed in the United States of America

For Ilona, Arthur, and David, who'll have to make the best of it. And for Lisa, Nina, Tamara and their partners, who, being slightly older, are well on their way to doing exactly that.

Contents

PART ONE
Converging Changes: Economy, Civil Society and the State

PART TWO
Changing the Nature of the State

PART THREE
No Small Change

Illustrations

List of Figures

List of Tables

Acknowledgements

This book grows out of our 10-year-long joint efforts to examine the new economy. Over the years, we've discovered the importance of innovation (*No Small Change*, Macmillan Canada, 1993) and the emergence of a networked private economy (*Class Action*, Robert Davies Press, 1993). Dian then went on to explore the desperate fiscal plight of the advanced countries, especially Canada, which she wrote up in *The New Retirement: Financial Strategies for Life after Work* (Doubleday, 1999, 2nd ed. 2000). Now we're continuing that examination by looking in more depth at how the new technologies change the capacities of public sector institutions. The linchpin is the declining power of governments to tax, as well as the link to the continuing crisis of an aging workforce. But additionally, and more optimistically, there is also the exciting discovery of a burgeoning, networked civil society that is increasingly stealing the initiative from government on important questions dealing with globalization and networked politics in general. This book, though far from a comprehensive treatment, is a signal that not only is our system in crisis, *but that the tools and forces are at hand to enable us to work towards something quite new.*

This new level of social organization, like others before it, will represent a break with the past. As such, it offers the threat of loss as well as the opportunity for gain. How will it turn out? We're not sure—big box stores include at least minimal instructions in their knockdown furniture packages, but the future comes without any instructions and more than a little assembly required.

That the book has its current shape owes a lot to Charis Wahl, who helped shift its direction from something more narrowly focused and technologically grounded. Jean Kitchen also performed useful sorcery and sharp-eyed editing. A great deal of credit is due as well to some of Canada's most powerful thinkers in business and the voluntary sector, who took time out to listen and respond to the more radical ideas we put forward. Among that group, Bill Stinson, retired CEO of Canadian Pacific Ltd. was an early subscriber to the power and potential of the Internet. Special thanks go to Don Stewart, John Lane and Bob Sharkey (Chairman & CEO, VP Investments, and special advisor respectively) at Sun Life Financial Services, Linda Matthews and Greg Marlatt (COO and VP Investments) at Royal & Sun Alliance Insurance Company, and CC Huang, CEO of Johnson Inc.

Sue Dallhoff read and commented on an early draft from the standpoint of both a volunteer and a capital asset manager; Alan Westbrooke's sustained and unstinting enthusiasm was greatly appreciated, as were Tony Vescio's suggestions and encouragement. Roger Hall, John McNeill and Carl Beigie provided valuable and insightful comments on successive drafts. The text also benefited from an author's conversation with Stephen Blank, Lubin School of Business, Pace University, New York. Particular thanks are due to Tom Stinson at Nexfor, Inc., who volunteered both lively discussion and the title. Researchers Lorri Mackay and Lisa Cohen helped kill some dead ends while following other more productive leads.

The 'look' of the book—cover design and graphics—comes from the creative eye of John Conner, who strove mightily to make our ideas more visual, our charts less dense and easier to read. We are grateful.

Thanks are due to agencies of all kinds—government, inter-government, and non-government—whose publicly available research is helping to push forward on many fronts the transitions discussed here, as well as illuminating many current developments. We have worked together long enough to have gotten over our desire to throttle each other on a daily basis. As for any errors that remain, they are definitely the fault of my co-author....

Dian Cohen/Guy Stanley

September 2000

net results

The Internet—it's been around for 20 years. Now the big changes are starting to bite. Government's ability to tax you is declining—social programs can't be delivered and paid for. The Net has solutions, but they change the role of government and what it means to be a citizen.

PART ONE

Converging Changes:

*Economy, Civil Society and
the State*

Introduction

A Net Improvement?

"Faith and doubt both are needed, not as antagonists, but working side by side to take us around the unknown curve."

The century just ended, for all its war and horror, was the century in which mankind's material progress advanced further and faster than any previous age in history. This was particularly true for the advanced countries. Life expectancy at birth between 1900 and 1999 doubled from 40 years to 80 and "material wealth exploded beyond all previous human imagining."[i]

Now there's every sign that this progress can not only continue, but also, with the aid of new technologies, spread around the world. The main risks stem from too much prosperity (global warming) and too little equitable distribution—especially regarding drugs to fight the AIDS epidemic in Africa and more generally the 'digital divide' that appears to be curtailing full participation in the new technology.

This book is about the promise and potential inherent in the world economy at the close of the 20th century. It is about the impact of the Internet on government, in particular on government and social policy. Three main forces that now drive the world forward are also posing major challenges to government institutions, especially those at the national level. Those forces are globalization, the expansion of information technology, especially the World Wide Web, and the demographics of an aging work-force. The first two forces are propelling us forward ever more deeply into an information society. The demographic challenge underlines the need to make that transition as rapidly as possible - to reach the productivity performance required to meet the costs an aging population will impose. We also ring a warning alarm: the new information technologies upon which our prosperity and its future growth are based pose a profound challenge to the systems of governance now in place.

History is full of examples in which realities based on time-hallowed ideas are more or less violently trashed by new ideas that catch the imagination of the world. In the West, the idea of individual liberty overturned centuries of royal prerogative. In the former European empire of the Soviet Union, the idea of individual opportunity demolished 40 years of repression in the service of central planning.

Sometimes the ideas add to the sum of human happiness: individual freedom and responsible government fall into that category. Other examples proved lethal: fascism, Nazism and Marxist-Leninist communism. One certainty, though, is that the force of a new idea is one of the most powerful in all of nature. The Internet has become the latest such idea to set fire to the world's imagination—mention the Net and everything seems possible.

But how stable or orderly is a world organized around a global economy based on ideas—especially the ideas embedded in the technology of the Internet? Will it move humanity forward, or will Internet logic turn out to be as lethal or repressive in its consequences as other brave new views now consigned to the ragbag of humanity's historical mistakes?

This is no idle question. Stability and predictability give us the reference points we look for when measuring the significance of our own lives. "Such and such a firm has been in business for 100 years..." This is a favorite selling point, especially in Europe, where long experience is equated to mastery and reliability—in stark contrast to North America, where the old may be revered, but not actually respected. Not too surprisingly—for it is the NEW world, the word NEW is more powerful than any signifiers of long experience. New is exciting, hinting at possibilities only just being dreamed of. Yet the technologies that underpin globalization and the Internet are actually not new at all. Look at the list:[11]

• Airplanes—almost 100 years old	• Television—nearly 70 years old
• Telephones—more than 100 years old	• Computers—48 years old
• Automobiles—110 years old	• Internet—about 20 years old

The technology that has made our globalized world possible has been the wired tech of telecom augmented by television and jumbo jets. For business and government, that's only an extension of a revolution that began a century and a half ago with the invention of the telegraph, followed 40 years later by the telephone, and even that took 25 years to be assimilated into a national network. E-commerce is built around the networked computer. Yet companies have had computers since at least the 1970s. It's taken them 30 years to cyber up, and some of them needed Y2K fears to complete the job.

So why is it that we're feeling this shock of the new?

What's new is that all of a sudden, with all that technology accumulating for the last century, there's a new condition: ordinary individuals now have the same power to communicate as the 1,000 leading multinational corporations. *This is a social change, not just a technological one.* Millions and millions of ordinary people have a capability they didn't have before and they're learning how to use it. The number of new people on line is doubling every year. That's a new social and economic reality. Combined with the effects of economic liberalization, the new reality created by the Internet is that people have a lot more choices. People also feel they have a right to exercise those choices. And they *will* exercise their choices—no matter what. Where they are prevented or forbidden from doing so, they smash down the barriers and choose anyway. The only people who stand to lose in the face of this change are the rule makers—those whose success was built on restricting choice. Who makes the rules in private organizations? Middle-management bureaucrats. Who makes rules for society? Governments. The challenge of governing in the Internet Age is a challenge of adaptation.

Adaptation and Globalization

If the 1980s and 90s taught anything to the rich countries of the West it was that trade is about opportunity. North Americans embraced the opportunities that came with their free trade agreements and have benefited from a booming export business. Europe, with some trepidation, embraced a single market and a common currency within a space of five years.

But the rich countries did not really grasp that globalization is also about profound adaptation. It was the poorest countries with the weakest institutions that made this discovery, and have had to learn the hard way what adaptation can mean. Mexico, the formerly Communist Eastern European states—especially Poland, the Czech Republic and Hungary— are now, after a decade of reform, slowly building the foundations for a broad prosperity through trade liberalization. Other emerging market countries, those closer to Russia, or the less prosperous South Asian countries, have found that adaptation to globalization requires painful adjustments—ones that were long overdue and that their own political systems proved unable to bring off. Russia itself is a living illustration of the costs of adaptation delayed. The 80s and 90s proved that liberalization and globalization are beneficial, but you don't turn around a generation or more of despotism and perverse public policy in a few years.

Some idea of the scale and scope of change that accommodating the Internet demands can be gleaned from the adjustments made by North American business, where Internet penetration has come furthest and fastest. Its business models are new and they keep evolving. Even 10 years ago, while the management school textbooks were still telling managers to maximize value-added within the confines of their own firms, leading-edge North American companies in the real world were breaking their operations apart and outsourcing as much as they could. High-tech companies that lived by invention began partnering with others in the same or allied scientific fields. Business began creating networks of co-operation and even coined a new word for partnerships with rivals— "coopetition.[iii]"

The Net made everything work faster—and brought these fragmented companies to computer screens. 'Portal' strategies present an array of choices to Net users; sellers supply consumers directly—except that the actual manufacturers may be half a world away with an entirely different name. Dis-intermediation (where consumers and suppliers are brought into direct contact without a middle-man or intermediary), and re-intermediation (where a new intermediary replaces a standard retail chain) have all become new business models. eBay, the electronic auction site, is a new intermediary. Business models change at blinding speed. Bill Gates wasn't kidding when he said that Microsoft is always two years from extinction. The company is now battling for its life—not just against the US Justice Department and the breakup of the company, but against new business models and new computing environments that threaten its current business approach with death by irrelevance.

The challenge facing governments is the same but more difficult, because the ideas of responsiveness, competition and client value are far from governments' custodial culture of delay, obfuscation and power retention. There are three important dimensions to this: de-territorialization of the national structure and re-territorialization of the global and local legal structures, disintermediation of government programs, and the death of policy. These are very big changes.

The challenge goes beyond just plugging in the new technologies and tinkering around the edges. Rather, learning to cope in the new, rapidly evolving, global economy requires us to rethink our expectations of governments and the processes by which we run them. Failing to do so could mean we won't get the full benefit of the new technologies, and we need them in order to continue to build prosperity and progress. But doing so will also require making some profound changes in many of the things we take for granted: entities as embedded in our political structures as the nation state and the welfare role that national governments now play.

In making this case, we trace the way the new technologies demolish many of the underlying concepts and capabilities of the welfare state that lay behind so many of the advances of the last century. And we suggest some new ways of thinking about the public sector that will enhance our mastery of the changes that confront it. A simple question, "What is the impact of the new technologies on taxation?" provides an example.

Taxes—the New Option to Pay or Not

Taxes are the basis of all civil society. The bedrock of citizenship is the obligation to pay taxes. For us, today, this obligation has national boundaries. We can move around freely *within* countries to find the locations in which the level of taxes—at least local taxes—we pay corresponds to the services we receive. If we have school-age children, we will move to areas where schools are good, traffic is controlled—probably somewhere in the suburbs. On the other hand, if the children have left home and we want to be close to evening attractions, we may sell the house and buy a townhouse or condominium downtown. Our local tax picture will change accordingly—our smaller accommodation compensates for the higher tax rates of living downtown.

The new technologies allow us to choose our *national* tax jurisdictions in the same way: they allow us to choose globally—without leaving home. The national borders no longer matter in this respect any more than municipal boundaries.

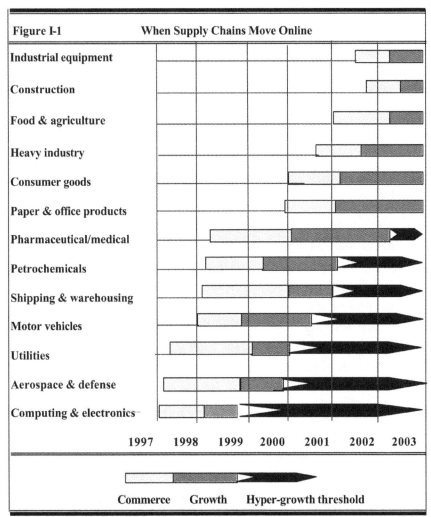

Figure I-1 — When Supply Chains Move Online

Source: Forrester Research in *The Economist, June 26, 1999*

Municipal taxes are usually about physical transactions (sales taxes collected at the local point of sale) and real estate taxes (based on your physical property). Rarely do cities collect income tax, because people can simply arrange their affairs to minimize their income tax liability with the cities—especially if they can create an office in the suburbs where no such tax is levied. The new technologies, as the nerves of a global economy, enable the same thing to occur with national income taxes.

The new technologies (1) create a global labor force and (2) allow it to self-organize so that it can pretty much decide what taxes it wants to pay where. Multinational companies have had this ability for a long time. What's new is that now virtually every service professional can have it—not just a few big players. By making every professional's national income tax burden as optional as state and local taxes, the new technologies and the global economy are creating a major social change and laying the foundations for a massive political change as well.

If we had the ability to decide whether to pay all or only some of the taxes demanded of us, what would happen to the welfare state and the millions of people who depend upon it? They expect 'free' education for their children, 'free' health and medical services for themselves and their families, access to 'free' training programs, and living expenses when they lose their job, have a baby, become disabled, and get old. How will government decide which social program will survive? What will replace the programs that are terminated? In other words, what about the acquired benefits that constitute the chief meaning of citizenship for millions of people?

Some new technology enthusiasts argue that the Internet can replace most of what government does now and the result will be a net gain in progress and social well-being. In other words, the Net may well destroy national tax systems, but we'll all be better off as a result. This position is sometimes called the California ideology, sometimes just radical personal or individual sovereignty. We almost agree—but not quite.

We still believe that public policy matters, but that the meanings and processes defining public policy have to change. The new technologies put back on the table a lot of what we take for granted (or used to) about the way humans live in groups. They force us to re-ask what the words 'family,' 'home,' 'work,' 'authority,' 'democracy,' 'rights' and 'obligations' mean, and how they should function now that we're all connected to each other.

Already, governments are debating and exploring how to tax the Internet. So far, there is an international moratorium on new 'Net taxes' because governments believe it to be in their interest to encourage e-commerce. But governments are also trying to extend existing taxes, such as sales taxes, to the Net so as not to disadvantage those with physical presence (bricks) and no virtual one (clicks). The implied squared circle of encouraging the new, but not at the expense of the old, underlines how governments are trapped between their own visions of the future and the claims of the past. This tension can only get worse as the Net expands, unless governments become a lot more willing to embrace change. The underlying question, "How can we tax the Net?" is the wrong question. Governments should be asking what public policy adjustments should be undertaken to match the private sector adjustment to the high-bandwidth globalization of today and tomorrow.

Globalization—the expansion of trade and investment worldwide—is both cause and effect of businesses earning money outside their home countries. National tax systems have had to adjust to this reality.[iv] As a technical possibility, e-commerce business transactions over the Internet can, for non-material items (like software, music, books, graphic designs, etc.) operate seamlessly within the Internet, never moving into physical space. Services of many kinds fit into this category—research, writing and editing to name a few. Most important, so do the very engines of e-commerce economic growth, the instruction sets that make the machines and computer programs work.

Businesses are changing how they are organized. They are building strategies to profit from the advantages of e-commerce: in so doing, companies are building different business models that operate planet-wide, 24 hours a day, seven days a week (24/7), more or less on their own. Not even as traditional and historically familiar a thing as money (i.e., national currency) is left unscathed by the Internet whirlwind.

Today, money is just another information device. Cash is not very interesting even to banks—they much prefer to store 'money' in digital form (bits and bytes) on their computers. Sci-fi author William Gibson understood this a decade ago; asked for a definition of cyberspace, a term he allegedly coined, he replied, "It's where the banks keep your money." In other words, money and high-value items can already trade on the Net in such a way as to make it well nigh impossible for tax authorities to tax. As more and more business goes global via the Internet, the obvious conclusion is that taxes in any particular jurisdiction will become significantly more optional than they are now.

So: what happens to the state, social programs and citizenship itself as information technology advances? We wrote this book explore that question.

What follows, we hope, will underline the fact that we're discussing a change as revolutionary as any in history. Some readers might conclude that many of our observations are destructive: for example, we show that the widespread application of these technologies kicks the props away from the idea that the state has a primary role in redistributing income. But we also find the nucleus of something quite new and surprisingly positive.

We found almost 10 years ago (*Class Action*, Robert Davies Press, 1993) that there was a new, networked economy ready to replace the industrial economy. We now find that there is a new, networked 'civil society' out there, ready to shoulder a great deal of the program burden that industrial-age governments used to take on. The members of this civil society are non-governmental voluntary and charitable organizations (NGOs) and intergovernmental agencies and organizations (IGOs) that are within the United Nations framework.

We think this new civil society represents the link between public policy and optional taxation. An in-depth, wide-ranging search of the Net and myriad conversations have convinced us that people will not only pay taxes but will also devote personal effort to maintaining and developing the health of their communities—if the context is right. The new economy's more voluntary taxation will allow people to match service needs and contributions. What's more, the Net itself is evolving the tools and links necessary to accomplish this.

However, we are also at pains to underline the fact that this degree of change is far from a simple, technical change in the way we govern ourselves. On the contrary, getting from here to there is as great a challenge as any in the past, one that will impact the very notion of citizenship itself. Just like the shift from the farm to the factory, or from the manor to the town, the shift away from the welfare state to a more active community-based citizenship will be a big social change. It's more like a tidal wave than an isolated event—a wave that can be forecast, even if it cannot be managed.

The Status of the State

These changes are coming on stream at a time when state-supplied social democracy is barely surviving. An aging workforce, globalization, and the new technologies have overwhelmed national markets and the controls that enabled the welfare state to flourish. Many will be unhappy that the welfare state is fading. Still, the reality is that governments are over-committed with undeliverable promises, and unable to raise the taxes their elaborate social programs demand.

Yet, like the absolute monarchs and feudal barons before them, the leaders of the national welfare states refuse to acknowledge the reality publicly, and continue to treat the old incarnation of the state as though it still had long life and a future ahead. The chief casualty of this denial tactic is government credibility. Citizens and voters are appalled, anxious, and angry about the public face of government superimposed on declining public services, broken promises, high taxes and mismanaged programs.

Internally, however, governments know very well they have to change. The trends are there for all to see, and numerous studies to this effect have been commissioned through multilateral agencies that policy-makers pay attention to.[V] We've benefited considerably from this research, a great deal of which is publicly available on the Internet.

More encouraging, in contrast to governments' generally nostalgic view of what their future role should be, is the growth of the civil society described above. Tens of thousands of voluntary groups with strong commitments to public affairs are emerging to operate in partnership with each other and with institutions to solve problems. These groups are a powerful counterweight to the commercial side of change—the e-commerce revolution we hear so much about. The emergence of this new civil society is part of an important process of change and adjustment to globalization and cyberspace and, most important, to a reinvigorated notion of citizenship.

Altered States, New Meanings

This is a book about change driven by technology. In the model of change that underpins the argument of the book, technology changes institutions by providing new capabilities that in turn alter our understanding of those institutions. We get used to institutions being able to do certain things. The institution comes to stand for a bundle of capabilities. Then along comes a new technology. By providing a new mix of capabilities, that technology changes meanings. But until we experience those changes ourselves, we continue to view the institution as embodying its old capabilities. Thus, many of the terms we use to discuss government, the state and citizenship have become encrusted with meanings that cry out for re-examination in light of the technological changes we are describing. The following selection will provide a broad indication of our case against the easy assumption of a protracted, continuous unfolding of the status quo.

Guy Stanley and Dian Cohen

The State and Government

In ordinary conversation, words like *the state* and *government* conjure up images of politicians, bureaucrats, judges and the military, policies, laws, orders and regulations, and to some extent, the political process. The terms thus begin to encroach on the word *polity*, which encompasses all the machinery needed to make and enforce political decisions.

In the physical world, the key to understanding the state and its government is the state's link to territory. The role of government is to manage the collective concerns of people on that territory. National defense is clearly a major concern. Beyond defense and foreign policy, we think of government's role as being to express national values and preferences as reflected by a more or less democratic election process.

Like national defense, rule making, regulation and enforcement are critical functions of government and the state over the territory it controls. Someone has to ensure that weights and measures are accurate, that the food supply is free of harmful bacteria and toxic chemicals, that consumers are adequately informed, that roads are safe to drive on, that drugs and cosmetic preparations are safe, etc. More recently, reflecting shifts in voter priorities, governments are taking more action to reduce stress on the natural environment.

The other aspect of government—social programs—includes those designed to help people through the hazards of life. This includes helping citizens to get a good education, to have access to adequate health care, to ensure income support after retirement or for those unable to work, and to help wage earners maintain their families when unemployment rises during fluctuations in the business cycle. For most countries, such social programs, including education, make up half to two-thirds the national expenditure. They are what we get for our taxes. The priorities we assign our tax-funded programs reflect national values—the underlying concerns and aspirations of the historic community that is the country.

But what is left of these bundles of significance if we decouple the market and its regulation from the boundaries of territory? Furthermore, what is left of these clusters of meaning if the state and government lose their predominant role in policy-making and program delivery? Yet that is exactly what the new information technologies do. They destroy one set of civil processes and enable others. They decouple economic activity from territory and have the power to substantially bypass government in policy-making. In so doing, they clearly change the significance of citizenship.

• *Public Goods and Market Failure*

Besides territory, a basic concept that underpins the government supply of social programs is that of 'market failure,' or the inability of markets to supply goods and services that people need. More generally, governments usually claim that when social fairness is at odds with efficiency, they have an obligation to intervene. This idea, embedded in the industrial age, no longer holds in the same way or to the same degree in an information economy. Not only, therefore, do the traditional concerns of government become unhitched from territory; neither do the easy assumptions about market failure hold any longer. Consequently, a different pattern of governing is called for—one that breaks with the practice of throwing publicly financed programs at perceived economic problems.

• *Public Debt and Capital Markets*

The ability of governments to govern depends on their ability to tax: that is, to convince or coerce people and businesses to pay the state to support its activities. But sometimes voters don't want to pay enough tax to support the programs offered by the state. When government spending is greater than tax revenue—in other words, when governments run a budgetary deficit— they must borrow to fund the difference. Borrowing to finance social programs links the programs to capital markets.

It used to be that when states borrowed from their own citizens to pay for 'public works' programs—like housing and road building (so-called capital projects)—such activity stimulated the economy by creating jobs and a belief in the security of employment. Citizens were encouraged to spend money, particularly on items such as cars and appliances—the 'consumer durables.' This in turn stimulated manufacturing.

But in today's global markets, governments compete for credit against the rest of the market. So anything one government does is simply discounted against the other investment opportunities a global market can offer. Government debt and even large trade deficits add to investor risk and therefore cause interest rates to rise. The rise in rates cancels out some or all of the expansionary effect of government spending. To quote from an Industry Canada research publication,[vi] "Countries are…losing the ability to manage their own macro-economies to attain domestic goals alone."

The conclusion is clear: states no longer have the capacity to manage their economic affairs as they did even a few years ago. Governments used to manage the level of national economic activity by fine tuning total demand in the economy through taxes— so-called demand-side policies. That was during the 20 or so years after World War II, before capital markets became truly international. Now, linking public debt to capital markets severely restricts the state's ability to manage aggregate demand through tax policy. Jobs have to come from private, not public, investment. The tax and transfer mechanisms that underpinned social democracy are no longer effective.

• *Macro-economic Policy*

Government taxing, borrowing and economic stimulus makes up what economists call macro-economic policy. In many economic models, macro policy operates according to rules that differ from those in which real people work, earn, spend, and save—in the micro-economy. There are two major reasons economists assume the macro-economy doesn't operate according to the rules for you and me: *lenders believe that governments will never declare bankruptcy and that governments can always raise taxes if necessary.* Lenders don't assume that individuals or firms—you and me—will never go bust; neither do they assume that individuals or firms can always raise money. But globalization and the Net render untenable the assumption that governments can always raise taxes—and therefore we should recognize that governments could, in effect, go bankrupt.

The recent history of advanced countries has been to eliminate net new borrowing and to begin program reforms that will reduce their long-run debt, thereby providing some comfort that they will not go bankrupt. Macro-economics, which used to be about devising fiscal policy to ensure steady growth and full employment, is now about getting out from under a mountain of debt and finding other revenue sources besides the income tax, which has become vulnerable to the discretion of high-income professionals. All countries must do this to stave off fiscal collapse.

A second observation is also appropriate. Failure to push on with speedy adoption of the new technologies could destabilize matters even more. Highly taxed and indebted countries need the productivity gains that flow from technology. Otherwise, the combination of demographics, globalization and the changes new technologies bring to others could force even some advanced countries over the edge—perhaps in just over a decade— and thus risk torpedoing the long boom the world needs to cope with its other problems.

• *Big Business*

For the discussion that follows, it's crucial to keep in the back of your mind that the bedrock of the welfare state economy was industrial, not informational. The main aim of enterprise was the transformation of raw material into physical goods.

That's not the primary focus of business today—now money is made and wealth created by manipulating information: creating and modifying machine code and instruction sets.

The effect of the Internet on business is still unfolding, but already it's clear that the shift to cyberspace obliterates geography and slashes distribution and co-ordination costs of organization. Both government and business in industrial nation-states used to have big bureaucracies. The bureaucracies assembled and analyzed information, and disseminated their analyses as the basis for business strategy and public policy. The high costs of that activity seemed to justify the centralization of power within large organizations.

Technological change and plunging information costs upset these arrangements. New information technologies that distributed information on networks made it cheap and widely accessible. Networked computers eliminated whole categories of employment in which middle managers developed, analyzed, classified, stored and retrieved masses of information. Without middle managers, organizations became flatter and leaner and more market-focused. Management switched from being an exercise in command and control to one of mutual evolution. The new, leaner networked corporation has become the backbone of a new global economy.

• *Globalization and its 'Re-norming' by the New Civil Society*

Globalization is what we call the process of trade and investment that creates and sustains a global economy. It has occurred on two levels—that of regions, such as the Americas, Europe, and Asia Pacific—and between those regions as well. Trade and investment across borders *within* those regions has been growing more rapidly than *among* those regions.

By the mid-1980s, it had become clear that for globalization to proceed, the international rules governing trade and investment had to be liberalized.

The trade talks known as the Uruguay Round achieved that and the World Trade Organization (WTO) came into effect in 1995 (succeeding the old General Agreement on Tariffs and Trade (GATT) secretariat). The WTO (*www.wto.org*) provides the place for governments to negotiate how fast trade liberalization will occur and how far it will go. It also provides mechanisms to ensure compliance with agreements already signed. *But here's the startling bit—almost as soon as the ink dried on the new arrangement, the new civil society forced the experts to rethink what they'd just agreed to.*

In a series of impressively coordinated demonstrations in key centers around the world, the new civil society forced the institutions of globalization to reconsider their newly agreed-upon emphasis on economic efficiency and to admit the validity of new norms and new standards. This is a notable achievement: one part of a global process of re-examining the standards of accepted conduct by government and big business.

The establishment of new standards of conduct by the politically and/or economically powerful grows out of the power of new technologies to change popular perceptions of what is attainable. Re-norming is an extension of the revolution of expectations following the diffusion of American movies throughout the developing world in the 1960s. The politics of re-norming are there for all to see in the struggles for democratic civil rights, in the identity politics of minorities, in the effort to redress past grievances with official apologies.

Ironically, among the most successful achievements of the critics of globalization is the building and maintenance of a new, more powerful international civil society. Using the power and potential of the new information technologies, global civic action groups have (since about 1995)

- won important gains towards new definitions of national sovereignty and human security;
- changed the model of military intervention and enforcement of human rights in many places around the globe;

- placed on the table challenging issues of global environmental management;
- obliged governments to rethink their positions on trade liberalization less than half a dozen years after one of the most protracted trade talks since World War II; and
- forced the World Bank and the International Monetary Fund to reconsider their strategies for financial bailouts and development assistance, in order to encourage more explicit anti-poverty measures.

Let us hasten to say that we don't necessarily agree with some NGO positions; nor do we think they are always meticulously argued. The point is, whether one agrees or not with the positions they adopt, these NGOs are succeeding in building something new—a popular mobilization of multinational proportions, a new political reality that would have been impossible without the Internet and other new information technologies.

• *The Net*

The Internet, or more correctly the whole 'Infocosm,' is the matrix of interconnectedness that will soon link us all together in too many ways to enumerate. Today, computers dominate the most important interactive networks, but the day is rapidly approaching when we won't be able to distinguish clearly between a computer, a telephone, a television and many other information appliances. The Net is the emerging web of connectivity that encircles the planet. Just as human conversation is about much, much more than doing deals, so too the Internet is not just about transactions. In fact, it was originally designed for collaboration and co-operation in pursuit of collective goals. This has important implications for social policy.

For the purposes of this book, the main point is to think of the Net as the web that connects every individual computer user on the planet to every other user. They can transmit, transform, store, forward, copy, and change information—in all its forms—at the click of a mouse or the touch of a keyboard. What 40 years ago was beyond the capability of huge, room-sized computers, and 20 years ago was beyond the capability of all but large companies with international links, today anyone with a computer and an Internet connection can do.

This new capacity of ordinary people is changing our understanding of the state, citizenship, collective action and, more specifically, social policy—what social democrats regard as the glue that holds societies and nations together. If you don't take the shift to cyberspace into account, there's no point in discussing public policy. But in considering the Net, you also have to consider that it, like the state and the economy, is evolving under pressure from its community of users. Its designers are us. There is no controlling monopolist and no controlling government to decide what the next infocosm generation will do.

• *The Concept of Community*

While the new technologies have rendered the welfare state obsolete, they have also strengthened the ability of communities to manage the public goods that must be under collective stewardship. These are goods that communities provide themselves by virtue of being communities. Language is one, but even more important is a general sense of social reciprocity. There's a distinction between the public goods a disinterested state provides as programs and plain old public-spirited generosity, or social reciprocity. The distinction is that social reciprocity, like language, needs no central authority to supply it.

They are both components of public life that enable communities and countries to function as such—the confidence that a random act of generosity will contribute to a virtuous circle of similar acts. (Contrast this with simple individual reciprocity, in which I will do something for you only if I know you will do something for me.) This is the chamber orchestra school of economic development: communities are healthy *because* they have orchestras, not the reverse. People getting together to do constructive things out of mutual enjoyment create healthy communities.

This type of public good is based on intangibles such as generosity and civic spirit—the gift culture, or "gift relationship," as British economist Richard Titmuss called it, which has been a critical element in the popularization of the World Wide Web. It was developed free, and it works because Internet hosts agree to use certain freely available protocols on their servers. This gift is what underpins the current commercial success of the Net. You can also see the same gift relationship at work in some chat rooms or newsgroups, and in the amazing amount of helpful free stuff that makes the World Wide Web so endlessly fascinating.

Indeed, the Napster phenomenon of an ongoing, worldwide community music swap-meet is but one of the many exciting possibilities that pop up all the time. (To be sure, people who swap copies of digitally recorded music to create their own CDs drive the music industry nuts. This community activity looks like theft to them—despite the fact that record sales are continuing to grow). We believe that this free stuff on the Net, and the potential for more, amounts to a fabulous treasure of community wealth in a new form. Community wealth bypasses our traditional categories of evaluation, but like all wealth it adds substantially to its users' freedom of action and capacity to get things done, as well as enjoyment and understanding of life. This same wealth is also available to strengthen and empower communities at the local level to deal more effectively with their community issues.

The Net Effect

The bottom line is this: the information revolution that eroded the barriers between countries and created the groundwork for a global economy can also rapidly move all-important civic activity to cyberspace. This revolution will be as profound as any of the other social changes in the turbulent and dynamic history of the west. Like them, this revolution offers real possibilities for human advancement. The source of those possibilities is the co-operative technologies of the Internet.

These new technologies are encouraging a new kind of polity to develop, one based on widespread public involvement. It is becoming massively effective at both international and local levels. The basis of that politics is voluntary NGOs, a multilateral UN and other intergovernmental agencies (IGOs) and civic organizations. These groups are the heart of the matter. They are rooted in local communities and operate through the new communications technologies. Although tax assisted, they are mainly supported through private contributions.

Through their efforts, the Net has a wealth of resources devoted to empowering individuals and focusing public scrutiny. It means that any politician—national leader, local leader or someone in between—can become the target of global attention in a heartbeat. Unlike the top-heavy, wastefully slow welfare state, this new polity not only leaps tall buildings at a single bound; it is a lot faster than a speeding bullet. It is too early to tell, but it looks to us like the kernel of the new, cyber-age governance.

The Challenge of Change

Taken together, the Net and the decline of the welfare state amount to a social change as dramatic as anything in the past. In particular, like these other revolutions, today's shift will change our concepts of work, wealth, and, most important, politics. If the welfare state is obsolete, what happens to income redistribution and the protection of the less fortunate? Herein lies the contemporary challenge of civil society: what to put in place of the welfare state. The question can be rephrased in more general terms—can we develop a politics based on eliminating or reducing the impact of negative social processes, namely those that create and perpetuate misery, oppression and disadvantage to those caught up in them? The answer seems to be yes. The point is that such negative processes are social artifacts and as such can be changed. The political process involved is less a matter of institutional arrangements, more a matter of re-norming polities.

Certain practices once considered tolerable if not exactly defensible are now vulnerable to the sharp light of intense global public scrutiny. Increasingly, 'naming and shaming' seems to be asserting itself as a legitimate element of both domestic and international political discourse, as a prelude to more substantial intervention, including public involvement. This is another indicator of the construction of a new civil society, one that aims to establish virtuous social processes around the planet. Unlike earlier conquests, this one has the potential to grow more powerful with each success by establishing virtuous, productive circles in place of vicious, destructive ones. Its main weapon is the penetration of new information technologies, which are now overwhelmingly associated with economic growth and participation in the global economy.

Nevertheless, although the future is bright with new promise, there are also some new threats on the horizon. At least two possible futures lie before us. One is worse than the present, unsustainable welfare state—an arbitrary, all-seeing surveillance state. The other—a new, achievement-oriented but compassionate civil society—offers the prospect of greater prosperity and justice.

This book focuses on the latter, but we touch on the bleaker scenario as well. One of the biggest question marks concerns the willingness of the state to see itself becoming a less central actor in the system. A particularly troubling legacy of the welfare state may turn out to be its claims of omnicompetence. For the fact is, the national state as we currently think of it is both powerless and not competent enough to change either the tides or the future. Yet this hardly squares with current ideologies about government and the reach of politics.

The possibilities and options for running this networked, globalized world of ours are still evolving, and there will inevitably be mistakes made along the way. But one thing is already clear: this new technology offers the promise of a world in which democracy operates not only within countries but among countries as well. Achieving that promise is one of most significant challenges facing us today. That should be the goal that the new, information-era public sector strives to achieve.

What Follows

It's been difficult to organize this story in a straight-line fashion. Here's what you're about to read: Part One brings us up to today—Chapter 1 charts the evolution of the global, weightless economy and its impact on organizations. Chapter 2 describes in more detail the rise of the new civil society and some new social processes that the Internet makes possible. Chapter 3 examines the welfare state. Chapter 4 describes the reaction of the welfare state to these new pressures.

Part Two looks in more detail at the underlying concepts of public policy-making and underlines the challenge to them posed by the widespread penetration of new information technologies. Chapter 5 examines how they unhook the state from its geographic base — 'de-territorialization.' Chapters 6 and 7 dig into programs and policies, and Chapter 8 proposes an approach for restoring legitimacy for state action. Part Three looks at the challenge of change. Chapter 9 briefly surveys other revolutions in the development of the state and looks at the continued relevance of Britain's successful transformation in the middle of the 19th century. Chapter 10 summarizes the results of our reflection.

Chapter 1

Global Firms, Weightless Economy

> "For society, the Internet's a wonderful thing, but for capitalists, it's probably a net negative."
>
> – Warren Buffett,
> Chief Executive, Berkshire Hathaway,
> the most expensive stock on US markets

Globalization has created and is itself the creation of a dramatically new kind of economy in which the use and transformation of information, not raw materials, is the basis of all economic activity.

This new economy operates according to economic laws that are quite different from the industrial economy upon whose base it was erected. It can't survive on national markets—it needs global markets to grow. Low barriers to global trade and investment are crucial to the ways world economic output is organized after two generations of post-war direct investment by giant multinational companies. So today companies put enormous emphasis on having the lowest and fewest barriers to trade and investment. They want rules allowing only minimal scope for any domestic government to take unilateral action in these areas. Governments, persuaded that the economic pie will be larger if states can agree to put their best offers on the table, are willing to make rules as transparent and pre-dictable as possible and to lower barriers to trade and investment as far as they feel able.

Liberalization encourages competition among companies, which in turn, invest abroad in search of strategic advantages, such as access to better, cheaper supplies, or broader, richer markets, and for defensive reasons as well as offensive ones. Since the second world war, as national economies have grown, and as companies have expanded outside their home markets, international trade has grown even more. International division of labor—regional specialization—has also increased as multinational investment in regional economies integrates production centers across national borders and makes them more specialized.

As the chart reproduced below shows, trade has outpaced domestic eco-nomic growth since the post-war recovery got underway. The resulting national interdependency is now the precondition for our prosperity. The motor creating that trade was foreign direct investment—cross-border investment in facilities, companies, branches, factories and laboratories and, more recently, telecommunications networks and equipment.

As well as leading this transforming process, companies have themselves been transformed by it. As the global economy evolved from the 1970s to the 1980s, business discovered the kind of organization they had to become to compete effectively in a witheringly tough environment: they transformed themselves from hierarchies to networks.

Corporations that were once tall and self-isolated, with information flow-ing uphill and power downhill, became flatter, more customer-driven, net-worked organizations. This explains the downsizing of the last 20 years, as well as the mergers, acquisitions, spinoffs, alliances, cross-licensing, joint venturing and other less formal agreements for cooperating among compa-nies or even divisions of competing companies. All in pursuit of profit that comes from offering customers what they want at lowest cost.

Figure 1.1   Trade and Output Growth

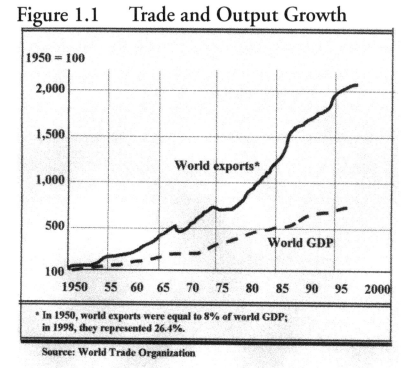

* In 1950, world exports were equal to 8% of world GDP;
in 1998, they represented 26.4%.

Source: World Trade Organization

Networks Mean Business

Networks are open; old-style industrial companies are closed. Networks are based on shared or distributed information; old-style industrial companies are based on hoarded information. Networks are radically non-hierarchical; old-style industrial companies are vertical. Networks are non-linear and simultaneous; old-style industrial companies are linear and phased. Networks can react and attack swiftly; old-style industrial companies' integrated 'value chains' cannot.

For many years, businesses analyzed themselves and their competitors in terms of their value chains — the steps needed to, say, bake the cake(s) the company sells. Value chains start with getting together the ingredients, finding a place or places to mix them together and bake, decorate and box them (i.e., take in raw materials, transform them into finished products) and then get them to the customer. This chain of activity also has to finance itself, organize marketing and promotion and develop customer service.

In the days before they discovered the Net and its technologies, companies tried to include within their walls as many links of the chain as they could, believing that such in-house activity was the key to efficient and effective output. It worked for a while, but networking across time and space made measured and phased production processes slow and uncompetitive. As businesses wired up, the model of best business practice changed: now they try to outsource all but what they believe they can do best—their so-called core competencies. Our cake company, for example, will get someone else to assemble the ingredients, sift the flour, and add the eggs. Its core expertise may lie in control of the distribution channels.

International companies, well before the trade liberalizing talks that dominated world diplomacy from the mid-1980s to the early 1990s, had already begun to abandon their branch-plant structures and to integrate production across international borders. Branch plants were common practice during the 1950s and 60s, when US companies first began expanding across the Atlantic into the UK and the new European Common Market. Typically, branch plants were smaller replicas of the home country operations, with smaller production runs of the same product lines. As a diagram, they look like the classic hierarchical organizational chart, with a top box for headquarters linked by vertical lines to a number of smaller boxes. The vertical lines represent control—information flowing upward and decisions flowing downwards. The smaller boxes represent different national branch plants—similar companies with similar product lines to those of the parent company. Noticeably absent are any horizontal lines between those branch plants.

Table 1.1	More Indicators of Global Interdependence			
Item	**Value at Current Prices**		**Annual Growth Rate**	
	$US billions		**%**	
	1996	**1998**	**1996**	**1998**
Cross-border mergers & Acquisitions	73.9	163	64.9	15.5
Sales of foreign affiliates	9,372	11,427	11.7	17.5
Total assets of foreign affiliates	11,246	14,620	8.8	19.7
Jobs for foreign affiliates ('000s)	30,941	35,074	4.9	10.9

Source: UNCTAD WIR Overview Table 5

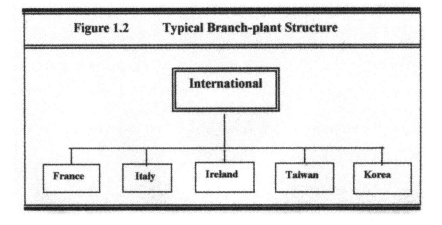

Figure 1.2   Typical Branch-plant Structure

The new, more integrated formats change the diagram to look like a spider web. The headquarters box is still there, but the branch plants have changed.

Instead of small, local production runs of the headquarters product lines for each national market, each plant now specializes in long runs of one or two components of the final product, as well as overseeing final assembly for a regional market of 200 million people or more. The plants are no longer branches. Instead, they are fully integrated components of a complex production system. A web of interconnections links the plants with each other, the parent headquarters and with outside suppliers. Gone is the national focus of the system.

As branch plants have gone, so too have the mini head offices. International management has now centralized even as production has decentralized. What has made this possible are the new information and computer technologies (ICTs) that link whole libraries of information dynamically across any distance. Gone too are the legions of middle managers who took care of coordinating the earlier system. Instead, computers organize the links. A B2B (business-to-business) virtual auctioneer takes care of internal pricing, and production is allocated by changing signals from the marketplace—dealers' inventories, customer purchases from the company Web site, changing currency values.

This new pattern of production depends on information and products being able to cross international borders risk-free with no surprises.[vii] The more a business distributes its operations around the globe, the greater its dependence on free trade and investment to make that strategy workable. The text box below portrays the relationship between integrated cross-border operations and trade liberalization. As cross-border integration deepens, the need for trade liberalization increases.

The web of connections among all this activity is what is known as a business network. They come in various shapes and sizes, use high-speed connections, have lots of

---

Background to Trade Liberalization: Company Strategy and Integration

When companies are organized with a headquarters and multinational branch plants, there is little cross-border integration of operations, and trade policy implements barriers at the border. Once outsourcing becomes a way of life, subsidiaries become specialized, integration across borders becomes stronger, accompanied by sector or specialized free trade. When a firm organizes itself into a network with a distributed value chain, it exhibits operational integration, with no barriers at the border.
Source: UNCTAD (1994) World Investment Report, p. 143

---

computers, and span borders. The cumulative effect has been to knit the countries of the world together into a single complex production platform built on intricate webs of high capacity fiber-optic cable. The business model is no longer a portfolio of enterprises run by a 'big picture' staff adding value through centralized procedures. Today's successful companies are knit together in networks composed of key suppliers, key customers and the transformation process. Many activities that were once accomplished within the company walls are now entirely or partly subcontracted to others who share company values and procedures but are more or less outside the formal company structure, like cousins in a family.

Networked companies have woven the world together in regional and global operations of hitherto unprecedented efficiency. Let's contrast the old industrial business model with the new: Ford Motors, for example, used to design next year's models at head office. If the designers and engineers were elsewhere in the world, designs were sent to where they were or they would travel to head office. The model was, for the most part, linear, and cars were made on a step-by-step basis: design, model, perfect, send the blueprints out to the branch plants for manufacture. Today, Ford Motors has an international network for producing its various models that saves millions of dollars and months of work. A designer in England may send drawings for next year's model to an engineer in Michigan, to work together making revisions on a jointly accessible computer screen. It may then go to Italy, where a computerized milling machine can turn out a clay or plastic foam model. Manufacturing facilities all over the world compete to produce one or more components for the model. The efficiency of the new organization has reduced turnaround time from conception to production line from 54 to 24 months, or in some cases even less.

Today's commercial world has plenty of 'productless producers' as well. For example, Dell Computers is a computerless computer maker—it doesn't make computers, it outsources their manufacture. But it does its own labels. It mans its toll-free numbers and Web sites to take the orders and pass them on to the manufacturers. They build the product to the customer's specifications, load it up with software and ship it to the consumer who has paid for it with a credit card, all over a phone line.

Stand-alone firms are increasingly dependent on other stand-alone firms, often in other countries, because networked organizations save both time and money. In the main regions of the world, dependence on foreign sourcing has increased by 50 per cent or more. For example, in the early 1970s, American companies relied on foreign sources for just 7 per cent of the components used to make their products. By the 1980s, they imported more than 13 per cent. Today, some 40 per cent of the chronic US trade deficit is made up of American companies trading with themselves. The UK imports more than 37 per cent, up from 16 per cent just 25 years ago. This interdependence will grow as e-commerce B2B supplier networks take off. Just recently, a dozen disparate American Fortune 500 companies, including Kellogg's, Bethlehem Steel, and Prudential Insurance pooled their buying power to create a $17 billion Internet purchasing consortium across several industries. New ones are being announced every week.

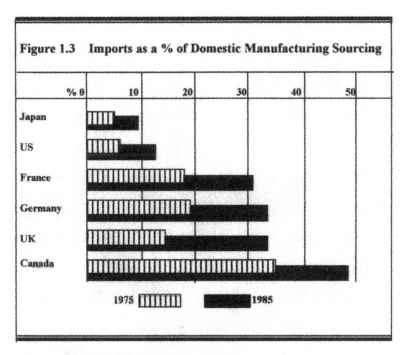

Figure 1.3 Imports as a % of Domestic Manufacturing Sourcing

Source: adapted from UNCTAD WIR 94 Table III.11

The advantages of this new business organization are many: equal or better product or service at far lower cost, faster time to markets and no inventory pile-ups. Suppliers get instant worldwide access to global markets through the big companies' international networks. For example, when the Mexican peso collapsed after that country's first year in NAFTA—probably the worst currency crisis in Mexico's history—Mexican branch plants that were net importers before the currency collapsed became net exporters within a few days of the currency slide. The company networks, aided by aggressive local managers, reorganized the flow of material in response to the new price signals: Mexican products became cheap to international buyers, thus spurring exports from Mexico.

From Silos to Nets

Networks have few authority stacks—chains of command by which increasingly costly or strategic decisions are taken as you move up the chain. Networks are open to outside participation. Networks enable people to inform themselves, to communicate with other people, to share and shape things of common interest, and to ignore what doesn't interest them. Applied across the country and across the world, the networking of companies is rapidly changing our way of life. From a society that organized production through big corporations, we are becoming a society in which the main work is now done in networks. Most important of all, today networks have become ubiquitous—via the Internet.

The Internet

Everybody today has heard of the Internet and, in North America and Western Europe, most people have access to it—at work, at school, through friends and family if they don't have a subscription themselves with an Internet Service Provider (ISP). The Internet as we have it now is a far cry from the nerdy playground for government scientists and academics that used to tie together mainframe computers at universities and government research establishments (the ARPANET). The story of the Internet is a fascinating tale of engineering ingenuity and unforeseen consequences.[viii] But the social and historical significance of the Net far outweighs its technical achievement. The Internet is the vehicle that makes possible all the changes we're living through—from the networked economy to the new civil society. How this network came to exist and to put so much capability in ordinary people's hands is a serendipitous tale. Government originally created the Net to meet the need for a global coordinating system that could withstand atomic war. The Net's redundant multi-point to multi-point architecture was conceived so that it had no center and therefore could not actually be killed or captured.

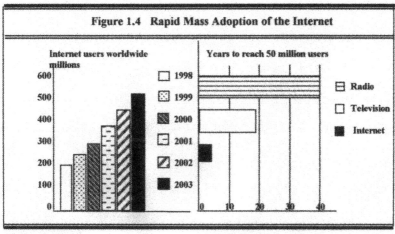

Figure 1.4 Rapid Mass Adoption of the Internet

Source: Nexfor, Inc.

But the Net was also designed back when mainframe computers were the rule and before the individually owned desktop computer was ever thought possible. The desktop computer, when it began to arrive in the early 1980s, was conceived as a device for individual use in creating texts, managing accounts and playing simple interactive games, like Pong and chess. The two technologies continued to evolve separately, until the advent of the World Wide Web made the Internet into a mass attraction. In 1993, when the first Web browser, Mosaic, came on the market, there were 63 Web servers in the world. By 1996 there were 16 million and the number of hosts has been doubling every year since. The incredible enabling properties of the Web—the first *new* mass social information technology since money—now underpin the workings of a whole new economy.

The Internet as Money

The Internet is definitely as revolutionary as money was when it was introduced thousands of years ago. Money was an improvement on barter: no longer did you have to look for someone who had what you wanted and wanted what you had. Money represented value, and a system developed to identify values of goods and services relative to one another: a cow is worth 100 units and so is a wife, for example. Once everyone agreed to the standard, trade could extend beyond the distance a person could walk. Whatever a society chose to be the unit of money—playing cards, stones, conch shells, precious metals—had to keep its value, so that people could store it (i.e., save) without worrying that when they later wanted to buy something, it would have lost value. The wider the geographic acceptance of the units, the greater its value to the trader. In today's jargon, money is the first technology to do these two things at once:

- embody collective or social knowledge (that is, we all recognize it and agree on its worth) and expectations (everyone in our society will accept it in exchange), and

- store it in distributed form (in wallets, cash drawers and safes) on a network (the people who use money as their daily medium of exchange.)

Money was thus the first technology of social information. We're so used to it as an exchange medium that we take for granted how elegantly simple an information device it is. Money registers an information exchange that is immediately understood by the parties to the transaction and the society to which they belong. The information describes 'value' given and received and stored throughout an economy. The only problem with physical money is that it can be lost, stolen or destroyed—a problem lessened when you separate the information that money represents from the physical form of that information. Whether paper or gold or conch shells embodied that information, money was the most efficient way to handle transactions until the advent of the networked computer.

The Internet is the second advance in social information technology. It is therefore far more than just a collection of semi-intelligent boxes linking together nerds and pornographers. The Internet is the first information technology to be more efficient than money. Money works on just one dimension of human affairs, that of the transaction. The Internet, as we shall see, works on at least two—the transaction and the gift. How so? Because unlike money, digital information can be freely given away without depletion—and because information can actually become more valuable the more people share it. (For example, widening the spread of knowledge that germs cause disease was the basis for improvement in public health.)

Besides its information-handling efficiency, the Internet is remarkable in another respect as well—it's uncontrollable and indestructible. That's another design feature that makes it so effective as the basis for an alternative civil and economic order (more on this later).

Networks and the Weightless Economy

The cumulative effect of these technological and organizational changes is the creation of an economy that runs on the instruction sets given to machines. These instruction sets encode the knowledge and imagination that managers put into developing a so-called business model—the formula the business uses to set up operations and make money. The competitive edge of the company comes from a dynamic loop of improvement: the business model must be novel in its approach to conducting business; the company must be capable of continuously improving the execution of the instruction sets; and the company must upgrade and innovate with the model to stay ahead of the competition. The sets of instruction are made up entirely of information; they have no material content. In substance they are nothing more than electrons moving within a magnetic field: they are weightless. Yet they govern the creation of added value. Hence economists and others today speak of the weightless economy, or the knowledge-based economy, or the information economy or even the de-materialized economy.

The point is that our civilization has crossed a threshold from being concerned with access to and transformation of raw materials to a new stage in which non-material instruction sets—their acquisition or development, and their implementation—determine who gets what, how much, how soon. In other words, nebulous bits and bytes now determine wealth creation. As the table below illustrates, the flows of technology payments now equal and can even exceed conventional trans-border investment flows.

Competing Today

Product quality, the key competitive factor during the Quality Revolution of the 1980s, is now just an essential condition for a business to stay alive. Every product must be perfect and perform flawlessly; the standard is zero defects. Key competitive variables today are the value of the company's patent base, the time it takes to get innovations to market, the ability to mass-customize the product to address the individual needs of its customer base, the turnaround time on order fulfillment, and the capacity to continually expand the range of products.

For example, if my company has its core competency in sports shoe design, I will want to segment that market as finely as I can to ensure that my shoe product responds to the differentiated demand of every sports shoe buyer. No more basic all-purpose tennis shoes. Instead, I make tennis shoes, running shoes, walking shoes, jogging shoes, shoes for different performance levels within each sport category. Each shoe is research-based with patentable scientific knowledge embedded in its look, feel and performance.

Some companies take the process a stage further and customize the scientific knowledge and design performance to the individual's unique physical characteristics. Fashion houses and bicycle manufacturers create top-quality products designed in real time explicitly for customers who have asked on-line for certain characteristics.

The industrial-value-chain business model is essentially extinct. The basis for that concept was to get big enough to reap the efficiency benefits of size and localized processing when transforming raw materials into finished products. Information economy businesses still benefit from scale efficiencies (order processing, shipping volumes, etc.). But the approach is based on specialization and focus, not doing every process in-house. The old, industrial-scale economies were achieved through making copies of material objects—the more copies you made over the same equipment, the less the cost per unit, up to a point. But digital products cost nothing to copy. So the old notion of achieving competitive advantage through scale economies—that is, being good at moving high volumes of material through heavy machinery—doesn't apply.

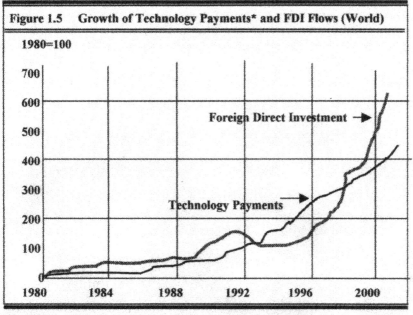

Figure 1.5　Growth of Technology Payments* and FDI Flows (World)

* licensing fees, etc.
Source: 1999 WIR Overview, UNCTAD, Figure 2, p.13

Instead, today, the new companies circulate information with the view to devising new and improved instruction sets and business models to sustain competitive advantage. The old value chains sought economies of scale and the ability to impose low costs on suppliers while extracting high prices from consumers. The new companies compete on the basis of innovation. To encourage innovation and adaptability, today's company is essentially broken into three separate but mutually reinforcing parts—research and development (R&D), transformation/manufacturing, and customer service. These parts are like fractals—they are each composed of the same three types of activity.

Each fractal is concerned with developing and implementing new instruction routines. R&D is where the new scientific knowledge is accumulated and transformed into protectable, or patentable, intellectual property, and then sold within the company network—or outside, if the discovery doesn't fit the company's plans. The transformation/manufacturing entity has to scan the activities of R&D shops globally—not just within the company network—on the hunt for new routines (i.e., programming instructions) to be incorporated into the manufacturing process to flesh out the company's product line. To be successful, this division must also maintain a strong link with a customer base that includes competitors as well as the company's own client service network.

The client service network is constantly looking for new products to match to the needs of its evolving customer base. You can break up these entities into smaller divisions, say by product line. Then the product line can be disassembled into the three functions of R&D, transformation and customer service, and so on.

Before its absorption by Pharmacia, Monsanto, for example, separated its life sciences business into three co-evolving product categories—food, nutrition and health—so that its agriculture and pharmaceutical divisions would work together on products that included such boundary-spanning categories as nutraceuticals—food products with scientifically provable health benefits.

Just in the last few years, business has been spectacularly successful in adjusting its practices to the reality of cyberspace. The most obvious networks are those discussed earlier, in which elements of the business are outsourced along a network of key suppliers, or the network is used to allow customers to track shipments directly, as Federal Express and UPS do.

Some Network Strategies

Businesses have also evolved other innovative strategies to create value through e-commerce. One of these is the Portal Strategy, a door or gateway that brings together links, items, information, and search engines to help visitors to the site find their way around cyberspace. Yahoo, for example, is one of the most successful portals, because of its comprehensive indexing and search engine. Its Web-presence has been augmented by virtual mail, conferencing and hosting services, to list but a few.

Another related strategy, which Yahoo is trying but eBay pioneered, is the *Auction* or marketplace site. The site provides a facility for trading. Discount broker Charles Schwab built this strategy into on-line trading pre-eminence. eBay itself is revolutionizing the way business is done by providing a spot price for everything as its auction site grows ever more vast. Yahoo and the bookseller Amazon.com have also begun expanding into auction activity. The extension of this strategy to financial services— especially the bond market—is the banking industry's worst nightmare.

Yet another strategy is based on *Virtual Community*—the creation of shared work and play space. America On Line (AOL), the world's largest Internet provider, is the master of this approach. Precursors included The Well, perhaps the most successful virtual community in the early days of bulletin boards, free-nets, etc. On-line co-operation offers incredible gains to participants. Of course AOL is a huge bazaar of activities and services.

But its thrust is to develop along the line of a virtual community for all communities of interest.

No matter how you break down today's companies and their strategies, the real product of each entity is tradable information: on new routines, new products, and changing customer needs. Each entity seeks to nurture and grow its own virtual communities of scientists (for the R&D entity), of potential contract manufacturers (for the transformation entity), and of the company's actual clients and their preferences (for the customer services entity). The information within the virtual communities can itself be valuable knowledge with a market value, tradable with that of other companies.

Networks Add Value By Growing

Just as the new company organizations bring into existence wholly new product categories, so they also bring into play wholly new dimensions of competition. Price and product quality are still important. But they take on new significance in the context of so-called network effects.

A network is a number of interconnected agents. Getting the right number, though, can be tricky. It's possible to have too few, in which case there's no advantage to the network. But you can also have too many, so that any benefit of membership is outweighed by the negative effects of overcrowding—can't get connected, get disconnected, etc. However, these negative effects can be held off by continually expanding the capacity of the network infrastructure. If the highways grow faster than the rate of new traffic growth, they remain pleasant to drive on. Or to take another example, if your ISP keeps upgrading its service so that it gets better as it gets larger, then the overcrowding effects will not occur.

People join networks so they can do something they couldn't do before—talk on the phone, hook up to the Net, co-ordinate their factories, and so on. Think, for example, of a phone network: the more people who are on the network, the more valuable it is, because you can talk to more people. The number of possible conversations grows geometrically with the addition of each new customer. Robert Metcalfe's[*] Law describes it: the value of a network increases with the square of the number of nodes. A 100-node network is therefore 10,000 times more useful than a 10-node network. As your network grows linearly, its value increases exponentially. If you're selling a networked product, this is critical: it means that the faster you grow your network, the faster still will grow the value of your franchise.

All knowledge products are network products—their value grows with the number of people who use them because of the information generated and shared. Consider the sports shoe example: whenever anybody buys a knowledge-based sports shoe, they provide some information about themselves and their sporting activity. They also report on the shoe's performance, and the company itself probably sponsors or cosponsors athletic events where the participants will use its product—thus adding additional value to the product. The more people who use that sports shoe, the more the company can learn about how that sports shoe is used, the faster and more accurately it can upgrade its instruction sets to produce new and improved products and business models. The better therefore is its competitive edge—and, as a result, the more value the market will confer on the company's share price, so that its market capitalization will grow.

The pinnacle of this approach is achieved when that company becomes the 'gold standard' of the industry. At that point people who don't own the product will want to buy it just because other people are buying it. The company has, at that point, achieved a critical mass of customers that will make the growth of its customer base self-sustaining. Microsoft achieved these kinds of rising returns beginning in the mid-1980s. Netscape achieved them with its browser product in the late 1990s. AOL achieved them with its radical pressure to expand in the 1990s to the

---

[*]Robert Metcalfe is the inventor of Ethernet, the most widely used networking technology in the world.

point where it was able to acquire the world's biggest multimedia company, Time Warner, early in 2000.

Contrast this with the industrial business model that is concerned with moving materials in an orderly way through the production process. Success was measured by economies of scale; but beyond a certain size, returns diminished, because the cost of each additional worker or machine outstripped the extra profit made from the extra production. Conversely, rising returns from networks are amazingly robust phenomena. Because there are virtually no marginal costs associated with making copies of digital products, expanding output is almost free.

Networks Can Also Wipe Out Value

Networks add value by growing, but they are also unstable. The instability arises from the way network access has to be priced if networks are to grow. They can only expand if the price paid by new members is less than the full value of membership. (Otherwise, by Metcalfe's Law, the price of network memberships would increase exponentially with each new member.) Because the price of access never covers the full value of the network, latecomers benefit more than original members. So early joiners have, in retrospect, overpaid in relation to the value the newcomers receive. This is what makes networks unstable. Early members dislike the arrival of latecomers, so they desert for other networks where they may receive latecomer benefits. Conversely, a new, start-up network may offer benefits the older networks can't match, and so may also attract new members. Even well established networks, then, are vulnerable to innovative competitors able to create a belief that their innovation will catch on.

Netscape strategists used network effects in a wholly original way. They deduced that perhaps new members should pay nothing—a network product can be given away until the critical mass is reached. At that point (in the absence of an equivalent competitor), people will gladly pay a membership fee closer to true economic value. Moreover, as the early joiners absorbed the benefits of early membership free, the network is more stable than it would otherwise have been—and therefore more valuable than if it had been established without the initial giveaway. Netscape's rising returns were echoed by Microsoft's catch-up efforts with the rival browser, Explorer. Microsoft's deep pockets led Netscape and AOL to combine so AOL's reach would expand faster—and with it, the Netscape browser (which by then had morphed into an automatic link to one of the best portals on the Net).

This network effect of rising returns is a crucial and distinctive element in the competitive environment of the weightless economy. It's a process of dynamic growth whose successful undertaking makes extraordinary demands on company management and on capital markets. The rising returns phenomenon is convulsive or explosive, and doesn't fit well with concepts of time that are linear, measured and carefully phased. Rising returns generate nanosecond, Internet-time-based competition.

Airlines as Networks

Competitive pressures have led some network industries in physical space to develop techniques of stabilizing networks. The airline industry, organized around proprietary terminals that act as network nodes in a hub-and-spoke system, has stabilized competition by linking networks with 'peers' while controlling sub-networks of feeder airlines. This has worked because international air transport still runs on bilateral agreements that prevent cabotage, the ability of foreign airlines to serve domestic routes of host countries. Can something similar happen if the Net is redesigned or ownership concentration increases? It's conceivable that parts of the commercial side of the Net could be controlled in some such way. Much depends on the way networks compensate each other for traffic sent along each others' lines. So far, a comprehensive arrangement between the networks that make up the Internet has proven elusive. As for the public uses of the Net—that would depend upon the readiness of the new civil society to defend its new-found power.

Networks Share Knowledge

Because reproduction in cyberspace is free (copying costs nothing and distribution is as free as e-mail), the Internet is particularly useful as a common area where people can work together and share ideas. One of the earliest manifestations of cyberspace collaboration is the open source movement, which distributes free code on the understanding that those who use it will also fix 'bugs' and contribute to developing the next phase of the program. The best-known example of an open source operating sys tem is PC-based LINUX software, which Finnish computer scientist Linus Torvalds created for common development together with members of a dedicated user group. Its advantage over other networking software is that it has superior flexibility and amazingly low cost—it is free for the downloading. Because the open source system effectively mobilizes the ingenuity of thousands of users, the software can become very solid very quickly and attract the development of many compatible applications.

Indeed, Microsoft used a quasi-open source approach by releasing enough of the Windows source code that developers could produce applications for Windows. The resulting explosion of new applications made the Windows system that much more valuable than its then arch-rival Apple, which kept a tight lid on its code and sought to control the development of all Apple-compatible applications. Two other examples of the cooperative power of the Net are Napster and Gnutella, Web-based technologies designed to allow fans to swap digitally recorded music, which challenged the entire structure of the multi-billion-dollar recording industry as a result.

Networks Respond to Networks

Networks are *reflexive*—that is, if they change the environment, they are themselves changed when that environment changes. As the Net attracts more e-business, it will come under increasing pressure to be more secure and more transaction oriented than it had to be when it was conceived as a way for nuclear war survivors to communicate. We're already seeing the Net evolve from essentially a dumb space with the intelligence at the periphery, to a more intelligent space with more intelligence located within the Net itself. For example, as Net traffic moves across networks with more carrying capacity, the owners of that capacity may build in some features that make it easier to identify messages by content type and sender. This would encourage market data collection, and would also make it easier to levy some taxes.

More generally, the property of reflexivity breaks an old engineering axiom that no machine can ever make another machine more complex than itself. Reflexivity allows machines like the Net to morph themselves through evolutionary change into a much more complex environment. In the industrial age, machines made machines. In the information age, machines evolve new, more complex, machines.

The Weightless Economy and its Challenge to Government

Taken together, the weightless economy, the networked global firm and the way it competes pose some basic challenges to national governments. One of the most basic challenges is simply measuring activity of such an economy. The move from physical atoms to electronic bits brings together categories long treated as separate in national economic statistics. In the 1930s and 40s, when the measures of national economic activity were being created, the following truths seemed self-evident:

- that national boundaries are identical with national economies;
- that goods and services are distinctly different outputs;
- that inventory gets used up;
- that direct investment goes into either real estate or machinery and equipment; and
- that trade and investment are quite distinct from each other.

Today, where digital products and services are concerned, none of these precepts is true.

Products and services have become indistinguishable—for example, software can be either a good or a service, depending on whether an accountant decides to expense it immediately (a service) or depreciate it over time (a good). Today, direct investment flows into many other things besides the old definitions of capital equipment—for many businesses, mailing lists and other data collected on a hard disk or file server are investments. Similarly, investment and consumption become difficult concepts to distinguish when it comes to sales of such items as computers and software. Information in the form of market data or financial information does not get used up, although it can rapidly become outdated.

As for trade and investment, the weightless economy blurs the distinction beyond recognition. For example, suppose the design of a North American version of a product is transferred to the Canadian partner of the German production firm. Should the design be valued at its import value, say, $100,000, or as a German asset upon which royalties will be paid over the life of the design and the value of the products into which it is incorporated? The first treats the design as a traded article; the second treats it as a foreign investment. All this makes it difficult to measure national output correctly. Yet gross domestic product (GDP) growth is a key variable for many government decisions and also may affect revenue-sharing among different levels of government.

As well, the capacity of Internet technology doubles every 18 months; that's why computer equipment prices decline so steeply over any two-year period. This makes it difficult for government statisticians to construct industry indexes that are really comparable year after year. This in turn makes productivity changes difficult to measure. Similarly, the massive quantities of private data that an information economy generates can overwhelm government statistical machinery. For example, when the US Bureau of Economic Analysis used supermarket checkout data to track consumer prices in just two metropolitan areas for a week, they found it necessary to process 1,200 items.[ix] Scaling up to a national-level survey using such data would be a Herculean chore whose costs might well outweigh the value of the information obtained.

Paradoxically, while governments' ability to measure national economic activity diminishes, their ability to track flows of information to and from our households may increase, thereby significantly enhancing the public's concerns about privacy.

The success of the technology may have an important constitutional impact: strengthening the trend towards making the executive branch of government much more powerful than the legislature, provinces and states more powerful than national governments and municipalities more powerful too. Why? Another by-product of this new capability is that the power of those with more responsibility for government programs and access to data increases relative to those who don't have this access. At the same time, as governments are losing control over the national economy, politicians are losing control over bureaucrats and national level authorities are losing effective power to lower levels. Meanwhile social agencies are building data bases of considerable economic value, were they ever to be commercialized. (Another key to this process, however, is the willingness of citizens to supply this data which, in turn, depends on confidence that it will used for good purpose and not otherwise.)

There's also a question about what kind of legislation is appropriate in a wired society that can operate through 'ambient computing;' i.e., with machines that are intelligent and can be programmed to confer certain social benefits. A lot of today's lawmaking can be embedded directly into the routines put into smart products—for example, cars that won't start if their drivers are drunk, or car radios that won't function when detached from the automobile. Should governments simply mandate such solutions as part of any legislative attacks on drunk driving or petty theft?

Property Rights

Government is often said to have a comparative advantage when it comes to enforcing property rights. But that advantage is based on being able to enforce in practice the distinctions policy makers make in law. For example, should patents or copyright be the vehicle of choice for protecting software? Most governments opt for copyright on grounds that software is generally based on the use of commonly known tools to express ideas. Ideas should not themselves be copyright protected. Result: different spreadsheets are protected, but no one spreadsheet can be protected at the expense of the other varieties. Patents, however, do protect original ideas. In fact, they confer a temporary monopoly on their inventor. In the US, you can now (since 1998) patent e-commerce business models such as Open Market's marketing and payment system, Priceline.com's reverse auction and more. This means that you *can* patent a mathematical formula as long as it is embedded intrinsically in a specific business process that is computer-dependent.[x]

Remember that the Net is a social information technology, like money. Money needed territory in which to circulate; governments could enhance the usefulness of money by exercising territorial control and (eventually) learning to manage the money supply that circulated within the territory. Another critical aspect of the separation of countries and their economies is the separation of wealth creation from the power to tax it — a theme we take up in more detail in Chapter 4. The key point is that the Internet and cyberspace are beyond territory. The value of the information contained there has an ambiguous relationship to government that still needs working out. The basic question is "What can government contribute to the management of cyberspace, apart from a context in which the efficiencies afforded by the technology can be shared and enjoyed?"

\#

Chapter 2

The Net and New Civil Processes in Society

"Humans are hard-wired for generosity."
—Mark Frauenfelder

If there are lots of books about the new global economy, there are relatively few about the rapidly emerging new civil society. This, as mentioned in the Introduction, is a new global alliance of NGOs and IGOs springing up to match the power and effectiveness of the world's global production platforms. It's big and it's growing fast. The UN Yearbook of International Organizations now lists 40,000 such organizations, a 30 per cent increase over last year.[xi] The groups are organized into 35,000 action areas with 150,000 links joining groups to groups overall.

Not very long ago most ordinary people lived and worked within a single set of borders, thought they were less informed than governments about most issues, and felt that governments could be trusted between periodic elections to settle issues in accordance with the public interest. Voters were represented but didn't participate directly in national politics, except through carefully controlled opportunities and institutions, such as elections, contributing to political parties, attending all-candidates debates, responding to opinion polls, etc. Now all that's changing.

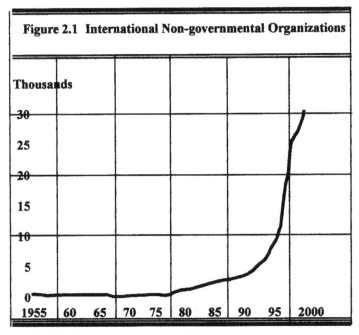

Figure 2.1 International Non-governmental Organizations

Source: Union of International Associations

The internal barriers to populist government were mainly related to the costs of finding out what was happening and participating in such a complex political process. Now the Internet has changed that by slashing the cost of public participation. The notion that there's no point in getting involved because you can't make a difference anyway is no longer valid. Politics is much more accessible to people. Not surprising, then, that as the Net grows, so does populism. It's now the driving force of the new civil society.

Civil Action Groups

Even if we've not been directly involved, we have seen the new civil society in operation on our TV screens. Many of us have visited their mushrooming Web sites. Some of their most recent accomplishments include:

Stopping the Multilateral Accord on Investment in its tracks. The MAI amounted to a single set of rules by which all OECD countries would have opened their doors to foreign direct investment. To trade negotiators, the MAI simply reinforced principles already accepted by the signatories of the NAFTA and the Uruguay Round of the World Trade Organization. The trade negotiators hoped the MAI would be the critical mass needed to win over those countries that had so far balked at liberalizing foreign direct investment rules. But the NGOs' adroit use of new communications technology, especially the Internet, stopped the MAI cold.

Governments' traditional way of working takes a long time. Creating a document for public consumption is immensely time consuming. It has to be okayed by the policy people and the 'spinners' before it's released. Inevitably the document also has to be cast so as to avoid being misunderstood by competing interests inside and outside the government. The MAI supporters couldn't move faster and couldn't counter the arguments of its opponents. So the MAI died.

Ensuring the Signing of the Ottawa Land Mine Treaty. An even more instructive model is that of the Ottawa land mine treaty, signed in 1999.[xii] This was generally regarded as a symbolic gesture without much interest for security professionals. Wrongly, they felt they could co-opt civil action groups by inviting them to sit in on discussions as observers. So powerful was the intervention of the NGOs that they essentially divided the security establishment. So great was the political momentum they provided that they induced diplomatic officials jointly to push the strategic conference further than the officials had originally intended to go. The government department most strongly allied with the NGOs—Foreign Affairs—got the better of the Defense department that was not so well connected to the new civil action universe.

Winning the Battle in Seattle. The WTO Ministerial meeting in Seattle in December 1999 also provides a good test case. Government representatives—functionaries of boundary-focused communities—met in a single place to discuss rules for an orderly opening of those boundaries to the forces of market competition. Then they came up against the Infocosm, as protesters staged massive demonstrations and successfully disrupted the opening ceremonies. More important, protesters also launched their own media center Web site to provide on-the-spot news coverage, much of it in real-time streaming video and audio, as well as a portal of links to resources critiquing the WTO and the global industrial system.[xiii]

Unlike the well-circumscribed WTO delegates, the protesters constituted a wide-ranging boundless coalition of protest against the world-as-it-seems-to-them, and projected it onto the planet's media screens. The flow of information was decisive. Before the Seattle meeting, the WTO was a little known or understood collection of trade experts working quietly but earnestly on the rules for market opening. After the meeting, they were portrayed as a bunch of secretive and powerful men making the world safe for corporations and unsafe for citizens. More important, among protesters, a new reality—an international solidarity of complaint—had been created and solidified using the same gossamer communication webs linking the corporate giants.[xiv]

The military and international business created the Infocosm. In Seattle, the new, wired civil society took it over. The NGOs showed their strength by dominating the agenda of the conference opening, the so-called Millennium Round of the WTO. Similarly, the status-of-women conferences in Nairobi and Beijing have injected gender issues onto every multilateral agenda. Unlike national representatives, NGOs are non-elected and to some degree privately funded. Their legitimacy comes from their ability to put thousands of like-minded people into the streets at those conferences. Emerging buzzwords like 'civil society' reflect the power of NGOs in an Internet-guided global political process.

Outing the Privatization of Policy-Making

The implications of this new effectiveness go far beyond just the ability of civil action groups to put people in the streets. Their success reflects a major 'outing' of the public policy process. The roots of populist success lie in the destruction of the old process that had, over the years since World War II, gradually but successfully privatized public policy. The face of power, still all too evident in most countries, is now exposed to challenge from outside the charmed circle of common values and shared ideology. Politics, in the form of public participation fueled by moral and ethical concerns, is returning to public affairs.

For many years, single-issue interest groups have had political scientists worrying that the liberal democratic state has been locked in an on-going constitutional crisis since the end of World War II. At one level, the crisis is about the rise of pressure groups that can influence public policy without being part of government. They have replaced political parties as the main architects of national legislative coalitions in virtually every modern democracy. For example, nobody elected the Canadian Medical Association to make health policy. But it's as important an influence as Health Canada. Nobody expects the Business Council on National Issues to make economic policy. But its influence has shaped crucial economic legislation in Canada for many years. In the US, with its more open and accessible legislative system and campaign funding system, private lobbies are even more important in the legislative process.

Clearly, a huge un-elected sub-government wields enormous power in most democracies. Yet it has no official status. Traditionally, the public service was supposed to reconcile political favoritism and policy development. But in the half-century since World War II, political pressures have proven too powerful. Just about every G-7 country is plagued by major political scandals linked to the costs of campaigning and the privatization of policy-making.

Information is the Key to Power

The key to this balance of power is information. Those interest groups closest to the power can marshal specialized information most cost-effectively, thereby strengthening the case for favoritism. Public service generalists rarely have the necessary knowledge to do more than comment on the government context. So when specialist knowledge is cultivated at the regulatory level, often the regulatory agency comes to share the industry perspective. In some instances, it regulates for the industry, not for the public. There are many examples of so-called regulatory capture. In some countries, the state actually owned the industries in question. Often they laid claim to natural monopolies. The list includes banks, broadcasting agencies, telephone companies, airlines, doctors and unionized medical workers…a long roster.

The effect of regulatory capture by specialized interests who dominate an information flow is that politics easily turns into a pay-and-take exercise among a charmed circle of interests. Despite the prospects for success it seems to offer, it's a game that nobody wins for long and everybody loses sometime. Moreover, everybody becomes worse off the longer they play, because it is in no-one's interest to look after the whole. Instead, the need to balance the single interests politically becomes the dominant concern of policy makers. Since few, if any, of the decision makers have the specialized knowledge to judge the information provided by the interest groups, perceptions of balance come to provide a political definition of the public interest. The need for productivity must be balanced against the need for jobs, for example; the need for innovation must be balanced by the need for stability and orderly markets. And since there's no reality in this game except perception, whether by politicians or their electors, 'spin-doctoring' becomes more important than discussion.

'Institutionalizing' the New Civil Society

The European Commission is one of the most energetic governments trying to 'institutionalize' the new civil society into existing public policy processes. The Commission's 'vision' of a wired Europe explicitly includes a computer-literate and equipped electorate. Having access to the Net and to computers generally is emerging as an entitlement of EU citizenship. In October 1999 the EU organized the first-ever conference on civil society at the European level. Discussions focused on the boundary between consultative processes and political processes, and the opportunities that exist for regular inclusion in deliberations of the Economic and Social Committees. A Commission in-house think-tank, the Forward Studies Unit, draws attention to the new, more participative, context for government and urges the Commission to work positively with civil action networks and to encourage their development.

Democratic government is supposed to act as an agent of the people with respect to special interests. But in *this* system, governments become agents of special interests, and impose their perceptions of balance on the people. The result is a major crisis of government legitimacy, reflected in galloping public cynicism and collapsing confidence in government's ability to accomplish anything constructive over the long term. Indeed, it accounts in large measure for the shift in ordinary voters' expectations of government. Where government used to be widely expected to provide benefits, now it is expected to bring problems.

The new civil action groups are able to change this by giving ordinary electors an alternative source of specialized information that challenges the information head-start of the privatized policy machinery. Their ability to make that information rapidly accessible in ways that are instantly understandable also encourages people to participate. "Maybe I can't understand globalization—but I can understand 'child poverty,' or 'sweatshop wages' or 'multinational corporations undermining the safety of the food supply'." It doesn't matter whether the information used by such groups is really of equivalent quality to that of the insiders. It just has to be good enough to raise doubt and underline the regulatory capture effect. The new civic action groups are the first lines of attack on a dying political process, and they're succeeding in opening it up to broader participation.

The civic action group influence goes further than protest. For these groups are also the heart of a growing volunteer population that's increasingly taking policy implementation away from governments and other public authorities. Volunteers run food banks, help out at hospitals, and show children how to make productive use of their time. Their numbers are growing and their demands to move into more and more policy areas are also growing. Charter schools, for example, are arrows aimed at the heart of a public education establishment that has disappointed many parents. Corporate sponsorships of schools and youth groups are a response to the challenge of transition from school to work that public programs have been unable to develop. Community groups come together at international, national and local levels to help put things right.

They work to establish viable, positive social processes in place of negative ones. The new civil society is also pushing the frontiers of democracy by promoting voter turnouts, especially at the local level. They're working to establish 'smart' or 'digital' cities that can bring every eligible voter into the process. University-based and other software providers are helping them. New products include on-line petitions that are verifiable, and on-line voter software that enforces the integrity of voting lists while preserving voter confidentiality. The recent Arizona presidential primary included on-line voting, and projects to encourage the practice are ongoing in many countries.[xv]

The new economy has enabled many more people to accumulate sizeable fortunes at an earlier age than has been the case in the recent past. Many of them have turned their attention to voluntarily taking over responsibility for community life, something that has been left to governments (largely by default) for too long. At the global level as well, UN programs have now made way for explicit partnering with relief supply organizations that are largely staffed by volunteers. As a consequence, we're beginning to see conventional security analysts explore such notions as 'soft power' as the locus of the next developments in national security capability.

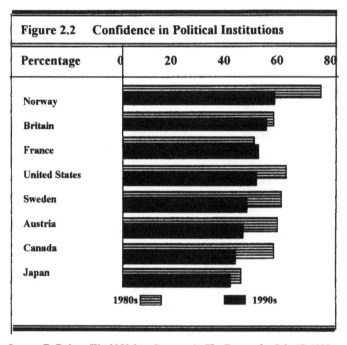

Figure 2.2   Confidence in Political Institutions

Source: R. Dalton, World Values Surveys, in *The Economist*, July 17, 1999

Taking Politics Back

Ordinary people, armed with the resources of the Internet, are taking back politics from the private special interests. Today, interest group/government lobby activity is under siege because citizens' groups have access to information and distribution channels that only the rich enjoyed a few years ago. It's now possible for an ordinarily competent adult to inform herself thoroughly on a vast range of public issues by spending a few hours on the Internet. By talking these things over with like-minded neighbors, and building more information through such combined searching and conversation, people can figure out ways of doing things better and then organizing to get things done that way.

This is a fundamental shift in the balance of costs and benefits of political action. Previously, governments found they had a cost advantage—it was cheaper for them to take command of the policy process. Now it's the other way round. It's now cheaper for ordinary people to be involved in civil action groups—and more expensive for governments to deal with well-informed individuals armed with detailed knowledge of a topic.

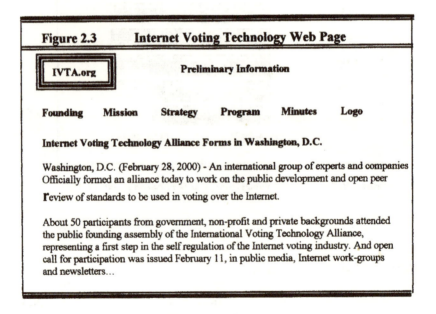

Figure 2.3   Internet Voting Technology Web Page

IVTA.org   Preliminary Information

Founding   Mission   Strategy   Program   Minutes   Logo

Internet Voting Technology Alliance Forms in Washington, D.C.

Washington, D.C. (February 28, 2000) - An international group of experts and companies Officially formed an alliance today to work on the public development and open peer review of standards to be used in voting over the Internet.

About 50 participants from government, non-profit and private backgrounds attended the public founding assembly of the International Voting Technology Alliance, representing a first step in the self regulation of the Internet voting industry. And open call for participation was issued February 11, in public media, Internet work-groups and newsletters...

National Government Functions Change

National governments still have a role, but nowadays it is neither unique nor privileged. Governments no longer monopolize or even enjoy much of an advantage in economic information. Government policy and financial capacity are withering because of permeable boundaries and falling information costs. Inevitably, NGOs will broaden their reach across nations and spread their understanding of the issues faster than hierarchically organized states can reply. So national governments' role is mainly to listen and see where they can alter the rules to make change a little easier to implement. The more they do this, the more mileage they'll get from their slender resources.

The nation-state still has a valuable franchise in that most citizens are still patriotic. For the most part, they're still sufficiently connected emotionally to their countries to fight and die for them. Few military experts believe the same can be said for a European army or even a UN rapid response force. An effective fighting force can, for the time being, still only be organized on a national basis. In addition, the state performs a useful administrative role. When it comes to adhering to international rules, it's easier if nation-states sign and organize compliance. Also, products or outputs such as laws are public goods that are uniquely supplied: the Supreme Court, the Justice Department, etc. co-operate on repairing, rebuilding and remodeling the legal system. Asked to choose (a false choice) between effective government and efficient markets, most people prefer effective government. Thus, comparative advantage in law-making still resides with the state, not the Net.

No State Monopoly on Policy

Yet the former policy monopoly of the state exists no longer. The original, constitutional political process involves parties serving as the mediators between the people and the state. Historically, the US is unique in the fragmented party structures that leave open so many opportunities for direct intervention by lobby groups and NGOs. Increasingly the US standard of openness is, in one way or another, becoming the norm in other countries' political processes as well. Systems are opening up worldwide.

There's a lot more idea-sharing and cross-country comparisons going on than ever before, through international agencies like the OECD and also via the Net. Now the policy development role has been pushed downstairs and out the door to the NGOs that organize themselves through the Internet. Proposed laws, especially in areas important to ordinary people, now need lots of advance consultation to win acceptance from everyday citizens. Courts too face competition. Alternative approaches to dispute settlement are part of the course in every law school today. Often parties to a dispute appreciate the fuzzier logic of Alternate Dispute Resolution because blame and compensation can be shared, and the scope of participation made more inclusive.

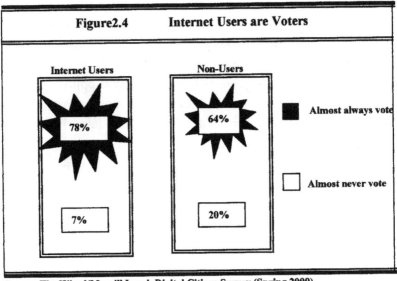

Figure2.4   **Internet Users are Voters**

Internet Users

Non-Users

78%

64%

■ Almost always vote

7%

20%

□ Almost never vote

Source: The Wired/Merrill Lynch Digital Citizen Survey (Spring 2000)

If political institutions in physical space are under pressure to change, what kind of institutional weight should we assign the Internet? It looks as though the Net has the ability to take up a good deal of the governance burden that national institutions can no longer handle.

The Net as City

If the Net is any kind of collectivity, it's a city. To the ancient philosophers, cities were the ultimate expression of human values. Aristotle wrote that Man is a social animal whose greatness is achieved in cities. The idea of a landed aristocrat or the dream of living in rural isolation (or our suburban communities) would have seemed retrograde to the ancients, for whom the city was the cornerstone of the life worth living.

Like a city, the Net derives its richness from its diversity. Jane Jacobs characterizes cities as "problems in organized complexity." She has identified four main elements of diversity that make a city richly rewarding and interesting: multi-purpose districts, short blocks, (that is, the ability to switch easily from one district to another), varieties of economic returns, and a dense concentration of people.

The Internet shares all these qualities. It is among the richest of all cities because of the infinite variety it holds. The hidden message of Metcalfe's Law cited earlier (networks grow in value with the square of the number of nodes) is that value comes from variety—the permutations and combinations made possible by diversity. Neighborhoods are interesting because you can discover things. The Net's the same.

French historian Fernand Braudel tells us that every point in the evolution of modern capitalism is marked by a dominant city. Venice, the leading city of the Mediterranean economy, was eclipsed with the discovery of the New World. Antwerp and Amsterdam dominated in the age of mercantilism. London was dominant in the age of steam and rail. More recently, it was New York's global financial center that broke down the Bretton Woods exchange rate restrictions and laid the foundations for the contemporary global economy.

But now even New York is being supplanted: the Internet and the other elements of the Infocosm are on the way to becoming the dominant city of dimensionless space, the center of economic, cultural and social activity. Moving human activity to the Net is equivalent to moving from the feudal manor to the city.

The New City's Dual Culture

Cities are about more than transactions. They have a dual nature that involves co-operation as well as competition. In the great cities, there's a feeling that goes beyond individual reciprocity: there's a sense of community. The Net, too, embodies a dual logic that's even more basic than e-commerce. Embodied in the fundamental architecture of the Internet is a technology that enables people to work together in pursuit of common aims. That was the intention of its 1940s designers. The Net is a culture based on community values—individual transactional values came half a century later.

How then does the Net affect the governance of the state? The Net has already weakened the conceptual pillars upon which the governance of the industrial state is based, especially the notions of natural monopoly and public goods [More of this in Chapter 6]. It has already weakened the ability of the state to tax while at the same time strengthening the potential contribution of civil society to build vibrant communities based on the Gift Culture introduced in the Introduction. But what is there embedded in the Internet and the wider Infocosm that affects the process of civil governing? How will those processes change as our use of the Internet becomes universal?

"Balance of Flows"

The answer lies in the link between the concept of 'civic' and the idea of the Net as a city. City management, as every city manager knows, is about balancing flows.[xvi] Too much coming in generates costs of overcrowding;

too much going out spells loss, decline and eventual ruin. Cities are nodes in a global network of flows. Cities use their jurisdictional powers to attract certain types of people and business—that's how they balance their populations with the services the residents are prepared to pay for. National governments have never worried about balancing flows; they are used to worrying about territories, boundaries, national defense, and raising taxes to finance things determined to be priorities. If they worried about flows, it was about controlling them or stopping them—not about balancing them.

In the last 10 years or so this has started to change. The European drive to create a single market for goods, services and people, adopting the necessary legislation and a single currency, is testimony to the renewed importance of economic flows and the need to reduce barriers as a measure of government effectiveness. At about the same time, North America completed its free trade arrangements between the US, Canada and Mexico. Unlike the EU arrangements, NAFTA leaves substantial border barriers in place, but North America is still friendlier to cross-border flows than it was before. At the multilateral level of the WTO, substantial progress was made in encouraging flows and reducing barriers, but more remains to be done. In particular, poor countries face (and impose) trade and investment barriers that sustain poverty and in general equate barriers with national sovereignty.

The Net itself is playing an effective role in forcing down barriers of cost and price to its own expansion, largely using the US and Canada as way stations to route connection fees through the lowest-cost routes in the system. If regions outside North America wish to expand their Internet flows faster, they must bring their prices into line with those in North America.

When governments agree on encouraging flows, the flows themselves develop a momentum and generate a self-reinforcing character. In the late 90s, those flows overwhelmed the financial systems of smaller Asian economies. They also helped to cripple the second largest economy in the world—Japan—until then, the success story of the 1970s and 80s. Indeed, the Asian economic disasters did more than any other single factor to call into question the process of globalization. As a consequence, some new civil society organizations (ironically, in view of their own use of information flows) are arguing for old barriers to be reinstated and new ones created. Indeed, they have already succeeded in legitimizing some trade barriers (on genetically modified food) that had been successfully negotiated away in the Uruguay Round of the WTO.

Importance of Flows

The success of the new civil society underscores the importance of flows. When trade negotiators focus too much on barriers, they ignore the *quality* of the flows. There's some protection in trade law for harmful surges in imports of goods (the safeguards clause) but so far, not much experience with anything similar for services. New regulations on genetically modified foods and other organisms were agreed upon at the Montreal conference in January 2000 and contained in the Treaty on Biodiversity. These are essentially just reporting requirements that will improve the flows of information among governments, producers and import/export firms. Still, seen in terms of flows, there's enough common ground between the different perspectives to continue forward.

The broader point is that momentum works the same way whether we're talking about products or policies. For just as companies with Network products try to generate enough momentum from their product sales—product flows to market—to make them the product standard, so public policies can have a similar effect. Governments can induce others to adopt similar policies and create new humanitarian standards, for example, because of the information flows of the new Infocosm.

Rising Returns and the Public Policy Process

When something becomes so popular that everyone wants one because everyone else has one, the bandwagon process generates increasing returns—usually in the form of revenues. Such processes are especially important on networks for two reasons: they can establish standards or norms, and they reinforce the network in the process. For example, once a critical mass of businesses began using the Windows operating system, those who did business with them also needed it if they wanted to share files to keep costs down. The Netscape Web browser was another such phenomenon.

Both examples show how rising returns can also stimulate co-development or co-evolution of other products or activities that add to the power of the Net. The popularity of Windows stimulated other suppliers to develop software for Windows that made it an even more essential investment. The popularity of the Netscape browser also affected the popularity of the Web and touched off a huge expansion that is still gaining momentum. The effect of rising returns also stimulates and is stimulated by the "open source" development approach. ("Open source" is the term given to a cooperative movement in which software is designed by the users and shared the users.) The more cool stuff that comes forward from "open source", the more other people want to contribute in some way. Rising returns create *de facto* standards or norms.

Consider this. Ninety per cent or more of personal computers run with Microsoft Windows as the operating system—the system that translates user inputs into computer activity. It's tempting to think that only Bill Gates benefited from his monopoly of the Windows operating system— but in fact the whole Net did, because more people joined the Web and are using it today, in part because of the ease of having a dominant standard.

We know that innovation is the key to prosperity and that it occurs when like-minded people gather to hit off each other in playful ways. Nets that encourage conversation also support innovation. Rising returns occur as an innovation becomes so successful that it is adopted as a standard. It's a natural process by which human beings choose tools that are communally useful. It's also how communities change and adopt new norms.

Social policy, too, can generate rising returns. Many private Web sites offering resources for social workers accept contributions and encourage resource sharing.[xvii] Others promote NGO involvement and contain resources for advocacy.[xviii] As networks become more powerful, they will promote more group work in these areas. Social workers, people in need, people interested in becoming active in their communities, can be more effective when they can leverage their efforts with others.

Sites that are helpful get recognized and become even more valuable as more people add their contributions.

Figure 2.5   Human Service Information Technology Applications Web Site

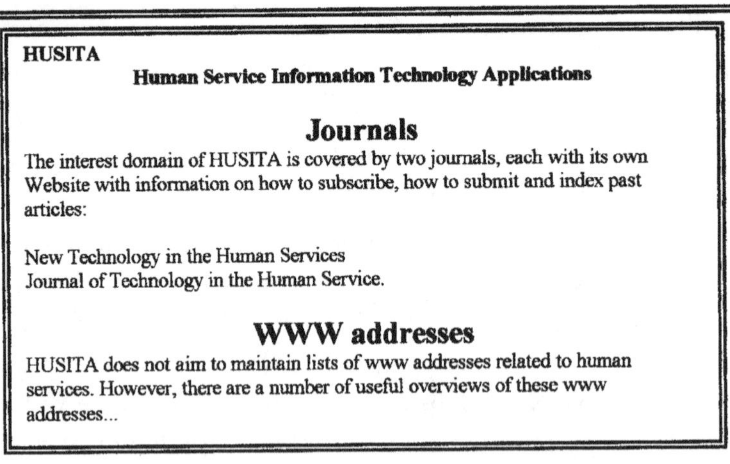

HUSITA
Human Service Information Technology Applications

Journals
The interest domain of HUSITA is covered by two journals, each with its own Website with information on how to subscribe, how to submit and index past articles:

New Technology in the Human Services
Journal of Technology in the Human Service.

WWW addresses
HUSITA does not aim to maintain lists of www addresses related to human services. However, there are a number of useful overviews of these www addresses...

The Net can bring to bear more knowledge on a problem than has ever been possible, and can mediate solutions as well. Ultimately, standardization occurs. A canon of fundamentally important concepts is created and discussed. The concepts become the basis for practical norms adopted by most practitioners.

For example, in Ontario, Canada, social welfare recipients have a hard time getting support to start a small business that, if successful, would pull that entrepreneur and perhaps others out of poverty. The difficulty arises because social agencies involved have competing perspectives and rarely talk to each other. Social welfare payments are still designed mainly for people who don't have incomes from gainful economic activity—in a sense they are payments for doing nothing. So they're not applicable for starting a business. Entrepreneurship loans are given to people who are already doing something and need to expand. They aren't available to people who are currently doing nothing. One agency considers it a waste of scarce resources to hand over funds to someone who might be gainfully employed. The other considers it a waste of scarce resources to hand over money to someone who might not.

So money and programs that could be used to help people move from inactivity to activity aren't available. Yet the stated goal of policy is to make people economically active as soon as possible. Governments that listen to stakeholder groups will learn about these anomalies and get rid of them. In doing so, they'll have a greater success rate. And, in the flexible and mobile world of cyberspace, they'll find themselves building a large community of people who want to do likewise. If the Ontario government reconsidered these programs in terms of positive flows, it would quickly become a potential model for other jurisdictions whose own NGOs would inform them of Ontario's success. The addition of other jurisdictions would gradually develop a momentum.

Lock-In: A Caveat

Along with rising returns goes another Net-related social process called, in e-commerce jargon, lock-in. This is the process whereby a supplier of a network product tries to keep customer loyalty by building in so-called switching costs so the customer stays on board. Regular doses of improvements or upgrades are part of it. But it can also include real barriers to competitors through carefully targeted incompatibilities. For example, the Netscape and the Microsoft Explorer browsers respond differently to different Web page codes. This makes it costlier for page developers to code for both browsers, which thereby encourages development for the one with the greatest market share. Certain computer programs, such as Java or Unix, have different versions depending on the supplier of software or hardware. Customer loyalty programs and equipment-specific training programs are other examples of how suppliers build in switching costs for their customers.

For NGOs, the equivalent of building in switching costs is to become the public standard on policy. Becoming an accrediting body is the preferred way to do it. For example, if membership in the American or Canadian Medical Association becomes mandatory to practice medicine, then the associations will have the power to enforce conformity with its views. Worse, the associations will have access to a coercive revenue stream (compulsory membership fees) that governments do not.

This actually happens in contemporary politics. Economist Mancur Olson has won acclaim with his model of the process. He tells us that the power of NGOs to aggregate public opinion is based in part on 'rational ignorance.' Paying dues and letting the association look after your public policy interests is cheaper than doing it yourself, especially in a world of information scarcity. But now, even though the information scarcity is gone, on specialized issues the rational ignorance logic probably remains valid in a world of information overload. Olson went further, suggesting that NGO gridlock could prevent governments from instituting free market policies that would lower consumer prices and boost productivity. Indeed, it wasn't until the leading industrial companies believed the prospect of gains was greater than their fear of loss that governments were able to embrace free trade expansion.

The prospect of interest group lock-in is changed but not necessarily lessened in a polity in which civil society plays a larger role than at present. This is especially true as NGOs become part of government program delivery, or even take over. To be sure, there's a powerful check and balancing mechanism in the voluntary nature of taxation. People will only contribute to or work for causes they believe in or from which they see some value. However, this doesn't reduce the need for vigilance and maybe legislative protection for association members and clients alike, especially since, as always, competition between NGOs will lead to increased supply at lower cost.

To take one example, the new openness arguably re-poses some old questions about the meaning of 'association' in the phrase 'freedom to associate.' This is less clear in North America where there are few, if any, restrictions on this freedom. But France, since 1901, has made a distinction between the freedom to associate and the freedom to establish an association as a legal entity with rights and obligations to its membership. Now it is revisiting the question with a view to liberalizing while still safeguarding the rights of members. While restrictions are probably not cost-effective to enforce, a program of voluntary certification could effectively ensure a basic standard of respect for members' privacy, financial and other interests. The point is that as the Net opens everything up even the most basic questions take on different meanings and new implications for public policy.

Rising returns and NGO competition can be encouraged by public policies. Policies could promote ease of entry and access to the affairs of the community, on-line and off. For example, laws and procedures that reduce barriers help make rising returns easier to stimulate and capture, and can also prevent NGOs from achieving too much power. In this connection, EU policies have begun to focus on the distinction between the consultative role of NGOs and the political roles of parties. This is an important file to follow.

Stocks and Flows

Public policy today is mainly about defining and protecting property rights. This reflects the historical concern with accumulated amounts (*stocks*) of territory and entitlements rather than *flows* of ideas, resources and people. Property rights *are* important—they are key to efficient market operation. But industrial society emphasized stocks of all kinds, including rights; the new environment requires emphasis on flows of all kinds. Sometimes, as in the case of such collective endeavors as open source technology or on-line music swap meets, industrial-style property rights may be sidestepped in favor of new business models. Nevertheless, it is particularly important that public policy also help to ensure the free flows that make up the collective wealth of the Web. Such spaces include social work libraries, labs, chat rooms, news groups, etc. Public information needs to be free and free information should be public. Laws that restrict access to statistical data should be carefully weighed against the benefits derived when communities of knowledge form and work together in cyberspace to suggest new ways of solving old, intractable problems. Ultimately, the new governance is about knowledge.

Knowledge Sharing

Working with networks means working in a context of distributed knowledge—knowledge that is shared among the group. Knowledge, in this sense, is based on a mixture of information and imagination that includes a commitment to action. Governments that want to promote imaginative community problem solving therefore have to share the information they collect and encourage its transformation into knowledge by the community.

Governments that do this can experience rising returns as communities see their usefulness. In so doing, they establish a norm that puts pressure on other governments to conform. Eventually, failure to get within an acceptable radius of the norm can result in devastating Infocosm scrutiny, with all the negative consequences that can entail. China and Singapore, for example, are under continual and relentless international pressure to conform to western standards on Internet use. Their failure to do so is presenting them with enormous diplomatic and opportunity costs. Ultimately their policies are not sustainable for technological reasons. Meanwhile, they continue to pay a price. It's true that this price is balanced by their openness to other flows, such as those of global capital. Yet these flows are inexorably pushing them towards western-style Web regimes. The problem will resolve itself as Chinese or Singaporean employees of multinational firms become increasingly dependent on company networks and interchanges with the global operations of their firms. The walls erected by government policy will effectively dissolve.

Barriers to Knowledge Sharing

A commitment to an information-sharing norm is difficult for any government to adopt for its own operation. In the set-up with which most governments are familiar, holding on to information is a better strategy for individuals than sharing it. In parliamentary systems, information is theoretically derived from access to power—the closer to power, the more information. Kings and their advisers supposedly knew more than the public. In that world, in which rewards went to those who made the King look good, they wanted to keep it that way. Premature divulging of information could, after all, have the opposite effect; therefore the King wanted to control all information release. The carry-over to our own day is that ministries continue to restrict information according to hierarchy.

Freedom of Information laws have had to be negotiated in order to stop governments from sitting on valuable information just because it could prove embarrassing.

In Congressional, US-style systems, information timing is also crucial because of the well-developed log-rolling process of legislative bargaining. The value of one's information depends upon what others know and when they are going to disclose it. In all systems, at all times, governments are enormous information accumulators. Their natural inclination is to store it or time it, but not to share it. The situation has become surreal in recent years as government organization has become more complex. In complex organizations, the top layer is often the last to know what decisions are being made—indeed no-one has a complete view of the whole.

Trust: The New Glue of the New Politics

Any discussion of information sharing leads inevitably to a discussion of trust. For communities to work, common values are *not* necessary, but confidence in the process *is*. In other words, people in successful communities must trust that there is tolerance in the exercise of different, even competing values. Organizations that run by constricting knowledge flows don't build trust. Consequently they are less able to generate organizational knowledge and innovate or diffuse innovation swiftly. Knowledge management on the Net is completely different. It relies on two-way information flows to build common understanding and, ultimately, trust.

This is new. Take customer relations. In old, vertical silo-type companies, customer relations was little more than a complaints window and an occasional focus group. Top management felt it was paid to understand the market and decide, on behalf of the shareholders, when and what the next innovation would be. No longer. Today's successful companies rely on customer communities for building their franchise and directing their innovative efforts. They ask their online customers to accept 'cookies' that, when placed in the client's browser, inform the company what pages and items attracted the customer's interest. In return for this, customers get targeted messages—an absence of irrelevant advertising—and are eligible for other benefits as well.

By sharing information and enabling clients to see the benefits of such sharing, sellers build confidence that they can be trusted. Commerce is enhanced, and in the most successful examples, the system may even lead to rising returns. General Motors' Saturn is perhaps the most celebrated example of this: today every company wants a relationship with its customers—the concept behind GM's approach has become a business norm.

What are the lessons for government in this? Government operations have only partially risen to the challenge of the new technologies. In particular, they are still trying to spin information as though they owned it. Gradually, however, national governments will become more like city governments. They will recognize that their tax base is fluid and depends on maintaining a high level of performance in the services their constituents are prepared to pay for. And they will recognize that information sharing is the surest way to build the trust and stability of their tax base. What's more, the slow learners will have the examples of the better governments constantly before them, setting new norms of effectiveness.

'Re-Purposing' Government

As Internet technology increases its presence, the national governments we know now will have to undergo major changes. Their taxing ability will erode, their function as income re-distributors will become untenable, and their monopoly on social policy making and program delivery will, for all practical purposes, come to an end. Governments will also have at their disposal the challenge of some new processes that could add enormously to their effectiveness. But the question remains: effectiveness at what?

The Net Result

Contemporary politics is about the ability to extract resources from the population and return them in the form of government programs. Ordinary people generally don't participate directly in this model of politics. It's based on an economy of information argument: only a few people can inform themselves adequately and it is they who should make the decisions. Social thinkers from Plato to Walter Lippman have agreed that only a golden few could do the day-to-day work of democracy, subject to the electorate at regular intervals. But others, like John Dewey and Hannah Arendt, believed that this was immoral, and that politics should rise above the day-to-day concerns about the 'gasworks' and reclaim some of our humanity through the joint pursuit of worthwhile common causes. In an international economy, with the penetration of Internet technology down to the level of even the individual contractor, an elite-dominated, exclusionary approach to politics is unsustainable.

The Internet has given politics back to ordinary people. The Net confers new power on anyone who wants it. Those who use that power and organize others can mobilize the many against the few on a broad basis that cuts across political frontiers in physical space. The on-line community helps overcome the problem of who speaks for the whole in physical-space communities.

This can happen in surprisingly mundane ways. For example, regulators and pharmaceutical companies may not fully disclose side effects of approved drugs—each for its own reasons. No matter. Specialized newsgroups of consumers and even physicians will quickly fill in with the information. Anyone interested in a medication can see all the information—the government regulators' messages, the manufacturer's claims and the reactions and warning of those with actual experience of the medications. Another example: company prospectuses and accounting data may omit some useful indicators of future performance. Investor discussion groups may point them out. The 'gift' relationships on the Internet allow us to hedge against system risk in physical space.

Groups on the Net have effectively organized serious, thoughtful grassroots lobbying efforts that can significantly affect how politics works in democracies. This information-rich context changes the role of citizens from passive to active. In this new context, government could become a catalyst, enabling people and communities to design their own public services based on their own real needs and in an information-rich environment, rather than an information-deprived one. But that government would be a conference of equals—not a conference of self-important officials with an eye to aggrandizing a department or drafting a sound bite for the evening news. And obviously, such a system would be far more operable at the local level than at an abstract national one. Governments aren't quite ready for this. They still stand in the way of more community problem-solving activity because, for obvious but illegitimate reasons, they are often more interested in defending their own interests than those of the public.

Hannah Arendt's critique of modern politics is that the industrial state is too preoccupied with materialism and science to tackle any subject freely. Now, some 25 years after her death, we have a tremendous number of new subjects, from sexual preferences to identity politics, and, emerging, a rough-and-tumble ethical debate on technological advance. In short, a new politics, rich in shared information, is now emerging. What's more, its agenda re-establishes ethics (in terms of what constitutes a 'good' society) as part of the political debate. The time is at hand for a new debate about the role of the state as an entity designed to help its citizens reach and enjoy their full potential within communities of many kinds. Mixing the Net and politics is re-opening a centuries-old discussion about how government can create the conditions for a collective good life through empowering people, rather than the reverse.

#

Chapter 3

The Welfare State Past & Present

"What is the point of buying the most expensive bed if you are going to lose sleep over how to pay for it?"

In most industrialized countries, the welfare state is taken for granted—at least as an ethical system, if not as a completely sustainable economic formula. For the average baby boomer, it's hard to imagine there was ever anything else. We grew up with it, and it's our model for thinking about the function and purpose of the state. Its scope was enormous: in its European version, it was almost invariably accompanied by the nationalization of the central bank and the major industries. Steel companies, the major rail and air transportation systems, the electrical utilities all became state-owned at one time or another. In some countries, any major industrial employer could find itself on the verge of nationalization, especially if business turned sour and massive layoffs loomed. Coal mining fell into this category in the 1950s. Some steel and car makers qualified in the 1960s. Although experience varied, virtually every country experienced a major reduction in the role of private ownership, designed to remove industrial operations from market disciplines.

The same thing happened to certain categories of professionals. Except in the United States, large numbers of doctors and nurses, for example, passed under state control through health-care programs, in which the state was the main paymaster. The formula for paying doctors was based on fees for "generally accepted" medical services. Gradually, doctors became more dependent on hospitals than private surgeries. Massive pools of insurance funding made this transition possible. In most countries, that money was essentially part of the tax system. In the US, it came in the form of company-managed mandatory health-care plans.

Generally, universities became the major beneficiaries of an extended education system. To encourage young adults to go on to higher education, and to soften the burden on families who might have expected their children to add to the family income after graduation from high school, financial support of various kinds was made available to undergraduates. Usually, this included a major subsidy from government to universities to cover the bulk of tuition costs. Students weren't the only beneficiaries. Science and engineering departments were recipients of heightened interest in their fields, stimulated by the Cold War. Additional state funding was found for the performing arts and national broadcasting systems.

Governments also regulated in the name of the public good. Before World War II, industries were generally regulated by sector—rail and air transport, pharmaceuticals, banks, investment dealers, etc. In the 1960s and 70s, government agencies were given mandates to intervene across all industries: occupational health and safety, consumer rights to information and redress, competition laws, and environmental legislation, to name but a few.

Programs designed to ensure income security for ordinary people accompanied all these measures. But only unemployment insurance was self-funded: welfare payments and pension plans were funded from general revenues on a so-called pay-as-you-go system. Those paying into the system financed those supported by the system, in the expectation that a more numerous and more prosperous succeeding generation would do the same for them. 'Universal access' became the programmatic embodiment of citizenship.

In the US there was greater organized opposition to the underlying rationale of the welfare state. Successive administrations brought forward the regulatory, educational and income support measures; but even firms whose sole customer was the government remained in private hands. Arts funding remained at arm's length, but the system of national science labs set up during the war was expanded to meet the Cold War challenge. The university-based science community eagerly participated, with the result that the US eventually achieved an unchallenged lead in sophisticated weaponry and defense systems, even though millions of Americans remained without access to health care that their NATO alliance partners enjoyed.

Under the welfare state, the sanctity of private property was breached; the capitalist ethic of a market-determined outcome based on competition was supplemented by safety nets designed to eliminate risk and promote the universal access ideal. The welfare state, it seemed, reconciled the demands of the industrial working class without destroying the positive parts of capitalism or political freedom.

By the mid-1960s, it seemed as though the struggle for production had been won and all that remained was to seek justice in redistributing income. Politics became a question of including the excluded in the benefits of the welfare state. Transforming the state itself was of little concern.

If there had been an ideological divide about laissez-faire or 'cowboy capitalism' after the 1920s, by the mid-1960s, there was overwhelming consensus in favor of the welfare state. American sociologist Daniel Bell coined the phrase 'the end of ideology' to capture that consensus:

> Few serious minds believe any longer than one can set down 'blueprints' and through 'social engineering' bring about a new utopia of social harmony. At the same time, the older 'counter-beliefs' have lost their intellectual force as well. Few 'classic' liberals insist

that the State should play no role in the economy, and few serious conservatives, at least in England and on the Continent, believe that the Welfare State is 'the road to serfdom.' In the Western world, therefore, there is a rough consensus among intellectuals on political issues: the acceptance of a Welfare State; the desirability of decentralized power; a system of mixed economy and of political pluralism.[xix]

Although its roots are traceable to earlier eras, the welfare state arose from two of the greatest catastrophes in history—the Great Depression of 1929 and its aftermath in World War II. The subsequent decline of the welfare state has occurred not because its humanistic ideals have been abandoned in favor of economic efficiency, but because globalization and demographics have made it unsustainable. Changes in international economic organization, largely a consequence of the prosperity the welfare state sustained, have kicked away props important to its survival. Still, the origins of the welfare state are important because they contain the seeds of its vulnerability to contemporary economic forces and they explain the emotional commitment this form of government engenders from its citizens.

Where the Welfare State Came From

The strength of the mid-20th century consensus was directly correlated to how complete the collapse of the old laissez-faire system seemed to those who had experienced it. People growing up in the newly industrializing society prior to 1929 were raised to believe that free enterprise and open markets offered prosperity for all those who worked hard and saved regularly. The Great Depression, and in particular the collapse of the world banking system, came as a tremendous shock to ordinary people: it was life- threatening and terrifying. Not only were their lifetime savings wiped out, but there seemed absolutely no way of recouping the loss. The economy died. Jobs were not to be had for some 30 per cent of the work force. Prices collapsed, too. The authorities seemed no more able to cope than ordinary people. Absurdities abounded: farmers destroyed crops in the midst of hunger in order to raise prices that people could not afford to pay.

Democracy and market-based solutions alike suddenly seemed outdated and outclassed by newer, more powerful governments organized along totalitarian lines. In Central Europe and the Soviet Union, experiments in social organization seemed to be producing better outcomes for ordinary people, attracting millions to the concepts of central planning. The supposedly futuristic fascism of Mussolini and the apparently dynamic national mobilization of Germany under the National Socialists seemed to show the way to a revolutionary future. The Spanish civil war seemed a harbinger of an inevitable worldwide clash between the forces of a bankrupt and reactionary capitalism and the forces of totalitarianism. US President Franklin Delano Roosevelt addressed the fear head on, outlining a vision of a New Deal in which the state would ensure freedom from want and freedom from fear. When war came, it was the ideals of the New Deal, not pre-war capitalism that sustained the ordinary Depression-hardened men and women at war, eventually defeating Hitler and the Axis powers.

The New Social Contract

The World War II generation wanted a new social contract and they got it. Its most complete articulation was the Beveridge Plan in England, which established a National Health Service and undertook to provide economic security 'from cradle to grave' for all citizens. Accompanying the medical plan was a more universal scheme of national pensions, unemployment insurance and public education. The British welfare state made England, the first pioneer of industrial capitalism, the new front-runner of a form of capitalism that would make another Great Depression impossible. In the United States, there was to be no national health insurance, but there was a GI Bill that gave a college education to every member of the armed forces who could qualify.

National Planning

Fighting the war also shifted public opinion in favor of national planning. By 1940, citizens of countries allied to fight Germany and Italy had been issued ration books that governed their purchases of dairy products, meat, sugar and gasoline. A wartime 'prices and trade' board had been set up to oversee commercial transactions. A 'capital control' commission restricted the amount of money individuals and businesses could send or take out of the country. Governments created special 'victory' or 'war' bonds that could be purchased in installments through payroll deductions at work. Even children were organized to help with the war effort by having public schools allot time for scrap metal drives and for students to learn to knit afghans and wool socks.

By war's end, the victorious powers had evolved complex national economic planning systems to replace the prewar market economies. The war had been won, so it seemed, by extensive planning, by centrally directed organization to carry out common aims. In organizing the transition back to peacetime, the preponderance of economic wisdom was that government planning mindful of market forces could out-perform markets on their own. State economic intervention could fine tune consumer demand to ensure that the national economy reached its full production potential. Governments could also intervene at the micro-economic level to clear up 'market failures.' In other words, governments would provide for socially (or politically) desirable projects even if the market would not build them.

Keynes' New Economics

Economics, meanwhile, seemed to many of its practitioners to have finally plumbed the mysteries of the business cycle. Underpinning this new government role was a new economics, based on the work of John Maynard Keynes. Keynes' reputation among economists was built on what seemed to be a dazzling new approach, in which governments intervened to improve on market performance. Among the general public, Keynes' economic reputation was bolstered by his stock market acuity. As well, they lauded his observations as early as 1920 that the Versailles Treaty, which had ended World War I and supposedly created the basis for permanent peace, in fact laid the foundations for a new world war. His new economic theory included the proposition that national governments could get stronger economic performance if countries could be isolated from the direct influence of international money flows. In other words, central government could provide the stability that laissez-faire economies needed in order to generate full employment and steady economic growth without inflation—provided the flows of capital could be controlled.

In contrast to the laissez-faire position, which held that markets would always work efficiently as long as competition was vigorous, Keynes developed a sophisticated approach to managing national economies, which governments could accomplish through the tax system. The government would use its fiscal power to dampen booms by accumulating a budgetary surplus, and flatten downturns by running a deficit.

In other words, by raising taxes when the economy was operating at near its full capacity, government would take money out of the pockets of consumer and commercial spenders, thus forcing them to curb their demands for goods and services. If the economy went into recession, government would create programs (funded with the surplus they had acquired) or would reduce taxes—either way, providing the wherewithal for people to purchase goods and services. The subsequent increase in economic activity would lift the economy out of recession and back into happier times. If necessary, governments would borrow money to finance such programs: that is, they would deficit-spend. In addition, governments could manage the money supply so that there would never be so much money in circulation that prices would be bid up, nor so little that they would fall unduly.

A New World Order

Supporting the domestic Keynesian economies at the international level was a new world order, based on international agreements establishing new world trade rules. The new system was supposed to work as elegantly as its underlying concepts. The Bretton Woods Agreement fixed exchange rates and allowed countries to put controls on international capital flows. It also created the International Monetary Fund (IMF) to act as a lender of last resort and to help countries alter their exchange rates if necessary. The General Agreement on Tariffs and Trade (GATT) provided the rules and timetables for the reduction of tariffs, and the penalties for countries that didn't abide by them.

The expectation was that countries would trade openly and increasingly, but trade flows would adjust to fixed currency values, given that government policies were sheltered from the pressure of capital markets. In other words, a country could not import a great deal more from a trading partner than it exported to it, because it was bound by the fixed exchange rate system to keep its currency within a narrow band of value. Should such a trade imbalance occur, the government of the 'offending' chronically deficit[xx] country was obliged to either (1) raise taxes or interest rates to curb the demand for foreign goods, or (2) go to the IMF for permission to change its exchange rate. Raising taxes or interest rates had the effect of reducing the amount of income available for consumption or investment, raising unemployment and thereby slowing the economy sufficiently that trade imbalances were righted. The policy had the added 'benefit' of lowering wage rates, thereby making the offending country more competitive so it could export more in the future.

Governments intervened extensively in the micro-economy in those years. State-owned enterprises abounded. Controls on investment, including measures to direct investment into particular sectors of the economy, were by no means unusual. When voters decried the rising unemployment rates, governments devised trade barriers that made imports more expensive. Because the General Agreement on Tariffs and Trade precluded tariff increases, which had worsened the Great Depression, governments turned to regulatory barriers such as domestic technical standards for products and investment restrictions linked to domestic job creation.

The GATT liberalized trade in goods but did not cover trade in services or agriculture. Countries could establish their own rules for services, but this was not an issue in the post-war years, since law, accounting and medical services were provided locally, not internationally traded. However, farm products *were* traded, and the failure of the GATT signatories to agree on rules for trading in agriculture meant that governments could ignore the signals sent by the market for particular crops and volumes. In contrast to the industrial achievements of the welfare state—where some discipline against subsidization applied—the result was little short of disastrous for world agriculture, where there was no discipline until a start was made with a framework agricultural agreement set up as part of the WTO.[xxi]

Protection from offshore competition in both services and agriculture gave governments an aura of omni-competence in helping and protecting citizens from the excesses of the market place. For 25 years, from 1947 to 1972, the welfare state was tremendously successful. Britain, Western Europe, Canada, the United States, Australia and New Zealand all reached hitherto unprecedented levels of prosperity while offering income maintenance, old age pension systems and (in most countries) health insurance. In effect, they made good on the Allied wartime promise of 'freedom from want and freedom from fear.' The main beneficiaries of these programs were average middle-class families who saw (1) more and better schools, (2) affordable access to university, (3) freedom from fear of being wiped out by medical expenses, (4) guaranteed income maintenance after retirement, and (5) relatively generous unemployment benefits that meant seasonal workers or workers in remote areas could sustain themselves in the off seasons.

In addition to these benefits, governments also built massive hydroelectric installations, superhighways and air navigation systems that revolutionized transportation and supported economic modernization in all sectors, including the family farm. Even more remarkable, it was achieved in the teeth of advice from older schools of economists who said that it wouldn't work, that it couldn't be done, that no such equilibrium could be sustainable, that the long-run result would be inflation and national bankruptcy. Andrew Schonfeld, writing a survey of contemporary capitalism in the mid-1960s, observed:

> The performance of capitalism since the end of World War II has been so unexpectedly dazzling that it is hard for us to believe that the [inter-war] bleak and squalid system, which we knew, could, without some covert process of total destruction and regeneration, achieve so many desired objectives.[xxii]

The welfare state was considerably more comfortable than most social change. It tried to take the uncertainties out of industrial society and ensure that its benefits could be shared throughout society as a whole. Structurally, however, it depended on the primacy of the nation-state. Its underlying assumption was that national economies followed political boundaries and that the nation-state was in control of the national economy, which it managed using Keynesian principles. These would produce non-inflationary economic growth and full employment amidst a range of social programs to ensure lifelong economic security to every citizen. That's exactly what happened for more than a generation. Small wonder that baby boomers remember no other system of state governance. Small wonder too that the chief beneficiaries—middle-income earners—applauded so vigorously the many important lifestyle benefits that were provided below market cost. One of the difficulties of adapting to the information economy involves acknowledging that the conditions that created the welfare state no longer exist.

Globalization and the End of National Economies

More than 200 years after Adam Smith established the discipline of economics, economists are still divided about the circumstances and policies that best promote and sustain economic growth. Nevertheless, while specialists debate the details, there's widespread consensus that Smith's basic insight remains correct: prosperity depends on specialization and the size of the market. In practical terms, that means international trade and investment are necessary because they allow people and regions to focus on what they do best, trading with other people and regions for the things they want but don't produce as well themselves.

But there is a clear contradiction between gains from trade and the welfare state's belief in economic micro-management by national governments. In particular, the welfare state had a *political* preoccupation with preserving the status quo that contradicted the Keynesian logic of omni-competent national economic authorities. Not satisfied with focusing on full employment at the macro level, welfare state governments also tried to avoid the transitional unemployment that comes with letting go of things a country does less efficiently than the things it does best. This led to non-tariff barriers that severely (and mistakenly) constrained the pursuit of growth through international trade and investment. The whole-hearted pursuit of Keynesian principles and the desires of national governments to protect their economies from the vagaries of policies undertaken by other governments in other parts of the world led to stop-and-go policies that kept unemployment higher and needlessly prolonged. The counter-cyclical programs put in place to protect people from the risks of ordinary life were never enough. Government borrowing to finance these programs grew exponentially.

In the end, pressures for increased growth won out. Globalization—the vision of a worldwide marketplace larger and more dynamic than the multi-domestic vision of the post-war planners—supplanted the older arrangement. Globalization rewrote international rules to facilitate a vastly larger role for international trade and investment than had been envisaged under the post-war GATT and Bretton Woods arrangements. Partly, these developments occurred as a result of the successful post-war recovery. Partly, too, they occurred as capital sought to escape the consequences of constraining domestic policies.

All this — the pressure of technological change, especially the growth of information and computer technology—made today's globalization possible. The initial driving force was foreign direct investment by multinational enterprises, which had emerged as the engine of economic growth and rising living standards after World War II. For that investment to operate efficiently, however, countries had to decide to let the major currencies trade freely against each other. A full description of how this occurred is beyond the scope of this discussion. Here's a short one: because of three forces—Europe's economic recovery, the money sent overseas by the US to finance its NATO commitment, and US domestic banking rules, which limited domestic interest rates—billions of dollars circulated freely in Europe without any compelling reason to flow back to the States, mainly in the accounts of the multinationals.

Eventually, it became clear that the value of the dollars in foreign circulation far exceeded what the market could absorb through trade at official exchange rates. So much liquidity was now owned by private firms that they could sell more than the central banks would be able to buy without violating the fixed exchange rate band for their currency. The US could have devalued the dollar, but thought doing so would endanger its reserve currency role. The Europeans could have re-valued upwards. But that would have jeopardized export growth and thus employment.

By the early 1970s, it was clear that the necessary policy adjustments would not be made. As this realization gained force, several countries decided that, since they could choose whether to accept payment for goods shipped to America either in gold or US dollars, they would choose gold rather than run the risk of American dollars that were losing value because of inflation. The Americans, fearful of a run on their gold stocks, decided on drastic action. They announced that they would no longer exchange dollars for gold at the official rate. The price of gold over the next several years rose steadily from $42 an ounce to $600 (and now hovers around $300). The Canadian dollar, which had been fixed at 92 ½ American cents, rose to a premium over the US currency. Thus the fixed-exchange world ended, and a new world began in which currencies traded freely against each other, rates fluctuating according to supply and demand.[xxiii]

The collapse of fixed exchange rates broke down an important barrier between countries and markets: no longer were domestic monetary and fiscal policies isolated from international capital. Consequently, governments could no longer successfully maintain what they considered to be full employment by fine-tuning national demand through deficit spending and monetary policy. Traders could offset government policy by selling inflating currencies and accumulating strong ones.

An important lesson here is recognizing the length of time it takes for social transformation to imprint itself on people's consciousness. Thirty years ago, without anyone saying so and perhaps without many people realizing it, floating rates and freely trading currencies rendered unworkable the social contract underlying the Keynesian state.

Yet throughout the 1970s, national economic policies lagged behind the reality of open capital accounts. Governments were still making policy as though they had the same control over their national economies as they had had when their currencies were shielded from daily capital movements. So government spending continued to rise as a proportion of output, and budgetary deficits continued to accumulate.

It took 10 years of stagflation (an unhappy combination of zero or negative economic growth and inflation) for governments to realize that the best way to achieve stable exchange rates was to achieve stable domestic prices. The levers of choice became those of money supply (monetary policy), not taxation (fiscal policy). During this time, more and more economists were abandoning their belief that the welfare state could optimize economic growth by central planning: they argued instead that the welfare state had created supply bottlenecks by encouraging so many restrictive practices—and that non-inflationary growth could be achieved by eliminating these restrictions. By the 1980s, this argument was known as 'supply side' economics. Its adherents had come to power in Washington and Downing Street.

Finally, it took a war on inflation, led by the US Federal Reserve under Chairman Paul Volcker and encouraged by free market believers US President Ronald Reagan and British Prime Minister Margaret Thatcher, to defeat inflation, restore fiscal discipline and encourage national economies to operate as global free markets. The process of deregulation and privatizing state-owned enterprise dismantled much of the original welfare state and let the invisible hand of market forces replace the visible hand of public administration. The supply side treatment successfully attacked deficits, although government spending continued to increase. Ultimately, it was debt and inflation that killed the welfare state—just as its early critics predicted.

The Japanese Exception

As these developments were unfolding in the West, another country quietly emerged as a potential alternative model to what the Western powers were doing. Japan had evolved a system that seemed to offer a similar sense of security to its people. But the role of the government was that of an economic coordinator, not a designer and provider of social programs. As in the West, guarantees of full employment and old age security were the result of a bargain between governments, trade unions and companies. But the terms of the deal were different. The system enabled Japan to raise itself from the ashes of World War II to become the second largest economy in the world, the most innovative and productive manufacturing power on earth, especially in automotive products, and to capture an impressive technological lead in consumer electronics.

The key to the Japanese system seemed an intelligent use of administrative methods to both strengthen the efficiency of economic forces and also mobilize and motivate ordinary people to pull together in achieving national goals. Testimony to the success of that effort is 40 years or more of steadily rising disposable incomes, growing market share in manufactured products, and for 10 years, the position as one of the global economy's two creditor nations, blessed with what seemed to be one of the world's soundest currencies.

By the mid-1980s, Japan had to worry about its fiscal position. Nevertheless, until the early 1990s, Japan seemed a model to follow. In particular, Japan seemed to show that a partnership of government and corporate enterprise could provide steady, non-inflationary growth with full employment, rising living standards and a light social services sector. Its positive contrast in many respects to the western welfare state-ism, as well as North American cowboy capitalism, seemed to show that a consumer society could be built on corporate capitalism that blended social harmony, tradition and social cohesiveness with rising individualism. But one way the Japanese system operated was by severely restricting foreign investment and relying on domestically raised debt—multiplied by circulation through banks and companies—to finance economic growth. This can work in isolated domestic economies when the borrowers are also the lenders. But in a global economy, exclusive reliance on debt is courting disaster.

Debt is vulnerable to business downturns. Once Japan had grown into a global business power, it was exposed to downturns worldwide. When American markets tipped downwards and the yen/dollar exchange rate slid at the end of the 1980s, it signaled that Japanese assets were overvalued. Borrowing had to stop. Business had to cut back. Projects went on hold or were scrapped altogether. Realignments of exchange rates by Japan's regional trading partners only added to the burden. Japan's economy went dead and has yet to recover, ensnared in an impenetrable lattice of mutual debt among the banks and the major companies. Greater transparency and greater openness to foreign investment would provide more flexibility and an ample exit. But the Japanese state and its business community still cling to the shibboleths of a bygone world: namely that a trilateral bargain at the national level can still make things hum. Only gradually are the elements of that bargain slipping away—lifetime employment, relative isolation from foreign investment, inter-industry protectionism. But slip they must, if Japan is to regain its prosperous leadership of the Asian sphere.

Back in the West

Elsewhere, the failure of the tax and spend formula to ensure steady growth and full employment without inflation has done nothing to lessen its ethical appeal. Even in countries like New Zealand, the UK and the US, where enthusiastically supply-side governments held power throughout the 1980s, there remains widespread public conviction that the welfare-state framework is somehow ethically superior to a more liberal capitalist state that rewards individual initiative. Social democracy, far from being a spent force, is asserting itself despite the fundamental changes in the world economy that undermine the economic efficiency of the old Keynesian formula obsolete.

#

Chapter 4

The State Moves Sideways

"The worth of every conviction consists precisely in the steadfastness with which it is held."

As mentioned in earlier chapters, the private sector economy has been dramatically transformed in the last several years. This metamorphosis has undermined the state's capacity to control the domestic economy. The effect of these changes has also altered the meaning of jobs, authority and legitimacy in a way that has to put even more stress on the social democratic foundations of the postwar nation-state. When the demographics of an aging population are plugged into the mix, additional stress faces many welfare-state assumptions. Not surprisingly, governments are having difficulty coping with this challenge.

Changing Ideas: Jobs

In the distant agricultural past, there was no word for unemployment, because there were always chores to do on the farm. The crops grown and exchanged were determined by custom and feudal obligation, not by market prices. Even in towns at the same period, 'jobs' were organized according to crafts; guilds developed a range of restricted work practices to ensure that the master craftsman and his family—which also included apprentices—had plenty to do. Journeymen suffered, but simple mortality ensured that most journeymen could eventually become master craftsmen despite restrictions. The notion of 'job' was closer to our idea of 'project'—jobs kept coming to master craftsmen because of their position.

The advent of factory production changed this. Factories took the skills out of traditional craftsmanship. The meaning of a worker moved from that of a social category (peasant, apprentice, miller, etc.) to that of a 'hand.' Factory hands had a job at the factory. But its assembly-line methods meant that the hand performed only a part of the whole project—the old meaning of job was dissolved by a production process that divided the job once done by a single craftsman into a series of specialized movements performed by 'hands.' Thus, showing up at the plant and working on the line became the job—it was the only identifiable job you could point to.

Factory production uprooted centuries of tradition and set in motion a transformation of society from an essentially feudal organization of aristocrats, peasants and craftsmen into a modern organization with capitalists, factory owners, an urban working class, and governments that were based on middle-class democracy. The industrial job was originally a precarious position that paid badly and was performed in appalling circumstances. It evolved to the point that in all industrial societies after World War II, jobs had some kinship with property rights; there was some acknowledgment of 'citizenship in the plant' through works councils or in some instances 'co-determination' of the company. Wages were set through formal negotiations between employers and employees, either through company- and industry-wide collective negotiations, or in some cases, national-level bargaining arrangements. Jobs became demarcated on the shop floor and assigned through seniority. The ability to control the flow of work was a matter of negotiation between management and labor—with ultimately more power going to labor in return for higher levels of quality.

Accompanying changes at the factory and industry levels, the welfare state also embraced a number of policy goals directly linked to the concept of long-term industrial employment. 'Full employment' was one such commitment, to be achieved through fiscal policy. At the micro level, that is, at the level of the individual enterprise and its workers, the program chosen was Unemployment Insurance (UI) to ensure against loss of wages. This arrangement assumed the existence of an employer, an identifiable category of employment, and a measurable length of employment. The UI program was, in effect, a portion of wages compulsorily banked by the state to be returned to applicants who needed temporary assistance between jobs.

Because all work for wages was seen as basically similar, it was a one-size-fits-all program, administered and controlled in ways we expect from industrial-style government. Getting UI was like renewing a license from the Department of Motor Vehicles: masses of people completing paper-based applications, then lining up to speak to an administrator who explained rules that were the same for everyone. The measurements applied to the program were efficiency (throughput of applicants and outlays, turnaround time for processing,) and effectiveness (time between rehires, etc.). As well, because work was invariably local, the system was flexible enough to embrace local differences in job creation or type of job created. Workers would be encouraged to relocate if jobs matching their skills were migrating. Administrators could be flexible on the criteria about 'actively searching for work' if a region was classified as depressed for certain job categories.

Now all these assumptions are obsolete. Work is changing. Consider: what happens today if people don't work in factories, but work at home, on computers? What if they can work anywhere via modem—so-called tele-work? What if the 'job' no longer entails showing up at a set place for a set time, but is in fact now a 'project'? What if the pay per project is not a regular, hourly wage, but a lump sum that amounts to, in effect, a spot market price for particular skills at a particular time? The fact is that few of the concepts underlying the old unemployment insurance program actually fit the working conditions of a wired economy. The 'employer' may well be another freelance worker. The ultimate client may be further intermediated by a giant consulting firm. The workers on the project are not employees in any standard definition of the term. Nor are they location-bound: the 'product' may be a component of a project being put together in Milan or New York simultaneously, in which a specialized input was required from someone who happened to be living in Toronto at the time.

What is the appropriate amount for government to bank for this worker's UI? What are the appropriate payout rates? Under what circumstances can she claim it? Clearly, this type of job is not what the framers of most UI schemes had in mind. Yet information work has increased to the point where this kind of employment now claims a large and growing proportion of the work force, whereas the old, blue-collar assembly-line worker is diminishing steeply as a portion of the work force. When governments have turned to this matter, they have generally tried to impose regulations that reduced the freedom and flexibility of those in the part-time economy, often in the hope of shaking more tax revenue out of them. Meanwhile, in North America, pay in the information technology sector is shifting to include substantial amounts of equity in anticipation of a profitable stock market launch or stock price increase. In the US, where capital gains taxes are low and rules covering stock options sympathetic, such compensation is not only of significant potential value, but also taxable at rates far below the top marginal income tax rates. This new form of compensation has sprung up alongside the traditional concept of salary and benefits and, for many on the cutting edge of innovation, constitutes a far more attractive alternative.

Leaving aside the public policy implications, what about the human implications of this type of work? There are also some important changes here. The factory job was also a social occasion: it provided regular contact with other people who eventually formed a social group. The opportunities for peer interaction provide links

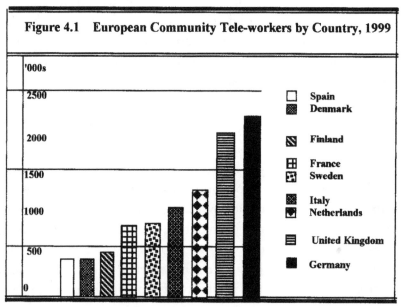

Figure 4.1   European Community Tele-workers by Country, 1999

Source: EcaTT Survey,1999

to a wider world in which concerns other than one's own can be shared and small satisfactions and triumphs celebrated. There's a mutual validation process at work that gives stability and meaning to life: a regularity that reduces uncertainty and allows people to build families and communities. Under this situation, lives have measure.[xxiv]

The new world of tele-work and entrepreneurship is different. There are satisfactions that come from accomplishment, of course. But these are more solitary. There are also more uncertainties. Jobs are not for life. Contracts are sometimes not paid on time. Sometimes they're not paid at all. Yet overall, the risks are less because one is less dependent on a single job, and the money is likely to be better because, in contrast to industrial jobs, information jobs require a lot of creativity and problem-solving ability. By definition, they can't be routine, because anything routine can be programmed. Because of these factors, however, information workers also need to have some community involvement and often do volunteering of some kind, either on-line or off-line. Indeed, where industrial workers felt insecure about their jobs and earnings and relatively secure about their communities, information workers are the reverse: money, while not certain, is not a big problem—but plugging into the community in a meaningful way is. To help, there is an expansion of the action groups that are fast becoming the basis for the new civil society.

Changing Ideas: Authority and Legitimacy

Just as the fundamental idea of what a job is has been altered by new technology and the organizational changes associated with it, so too are other social categories. What constitutes authority and its corollary, legitimacy, has also been changed. Management guru Peter Drucker has noted that modern industrial democracies have evolved with two sorts of authority-legitimacy structures. One is the political structure that sustains the state. It's governed by the principles of human rights and democratically enacted laws. The other is governed by the principle of competence. The competence principle is what sustains the legitimacy of management. In the context of the nation-state, management, however competent, is subject to the general framework of legitimacy that governs the state.

In Europe, the general framework of legitimacy also includes conferring status on employees apart from the compensation they obtain at the bargaining table. Employees are usually represented on the Board of Directors that oversees the general strategy of the company, and a complex web of rules and entitlements essentially makes it difficult for companies to easily shift jobs from one location to another. In North

America, collective bargaining is the rule: managers are freer to manage and it is rare for boards of directors to have employee representation. Instead, boards are expected to look after the interests of the shareholders first. That said, however, there is considerable public scrutiny on large companies and a vigorous civil law system that ensures a high level of corporate 'giving back to the community.' Besides civil law, a web of significant regulation exists to ensure that corporate functions are carried out according to norms that include employee and public safety. In the North American system, formal process is less important than performance and results, including measurable compliance with regulatory norms.

Like the welfare state, the postwar business system has its roots in the postwar settlement and memories of the Depression. Like the social democratic state itself, the subjection of the giant corporation to social control is largely a product of Franklin Roosevelt's New Deal and the Allied victory. Massive industrial actions in the auto industry in France and the US in the 1930s won the recognition of unions and collective bargaining. The reconstruction of Europe—divided between Soviet-dominated Communist 'worker states' and the West—underlined the importance of solving the question of the social status of industrial man. It was postwar West Germany that instituted the concept of the 'social market' in which workers, as well as owners and investors, had equal claims to authority in the workplace. This ideal was accepted in different degrees and instituted in different ways throughout the West. In line with the belief that nation-state governments could regulate the economy to improve on markets, the postwar business framework was designed to put in place institutions that would eliminate, or at least mitigate, the conflict between capital and labor and create real industrial democracy.

The results have never been perfect. Many of the principles that apply in political life don't apply on the job: freedom of speech, for instance, is often curtailed in the name of efficiency and loyalty. Freedom to live and work where one chooses is often overridden by management decisions about plant locations. Gender and racial equality of treatment is still an issue whenever it seems to conflict with the higher concern of competence.

Another issue is the relative balance of the claims that different stakeholders can make on an enterprise: management competence, to a shareholder, is often based on increased value and earnings per share. To a host community, it is often measured in terms of stability of employment and aid to community institutions, such as schools, sports teams and the like. In the industrial state of the 1960s and 70s—while capital markets were still mainly national markets—managers believed company survival depended on finding ways to equate the claims of stakeholders at the margin; social responsibility was an important business buzzword. The liberalization of capital markets, and in particular the advent of the leveraged buy-out (a technique that allows smaller firms to take over larger firms by borrowing on the strength of the combined new entity), returned emphasis to the importance of satisfying investors first.

Despite a half-century or so of industrial democracy in the West, no alternative ever emerged to replace the primacy of the competence principle in business. As long as the environment remains competitive, competence will always be the dominant test of legitimacy. Today, the amount of democracy in the workplace is an area of on-going negotiation between those who defend the competence principle and those who seek to apply standards of human rights. But even in this respect, the expansion of social performance criteria into the private-sector workplace is generally accomplished as an add-on rather than a substitute for the competence principle. Equal opportunity, for example, is usually defined as ensuring that all candidates receive fair consideration on the basis of competence, irrespective of irrelevant issues such as gender, skin color or religion. As well, the concept of management competence now generally includes getting the equity balance or the ecological balance right—not behaving as though the need for balance does not exist. To be sure, the *tests* for balance are linked to predefined outcomes, such as a rough equivalence between the racial and gender balance of a work force and its host population. But management competence in firms treats these as compliance issues: good managers meet or exceed performance expectation on financial, social and other targets (e.g. product quality, customer satisfaction, various process measures)—nothing more.

Pushback into the Public Sector

If the last 50 years taught business to incorporate social values into the competence principle, the most recent few years have seen a general push-back of the competence principle into the public sector. Insofar as political legitimacy is concerned, the principle of authority based on competence, not just compliance with democratic norms, has migrated to the political arena, especially for government programs.

Nowadays—in North America at least—public administration must do more than satisfy formal procedures; it must also be effective to be considered truly legitimate. Taxpayers want results for their money. Can the welfare-state system, which developed as an integral part of the industrial age, satisfy the competence tests of the information age? Not without such a radical makeover as to become unrecognizable for most practical purposes. The industrial state is really not competent to deal with the problems of the information age. Applying the test of competence to new areas will probably accelerate the trend to weakened government authority rather than strengthen it. At the same time, asserting competence in the old industrial state areas won't work either, because they are too often beside the point when it comes to information age concerns—as in the tele-work example cited above.

A critical problem facing all industrial states is that in their attempts to establish their competence, they're often chasing two hares at once rather than dealing with real issues. On the one hand, states are trying to assert their competence as masters of the old social democratic state. On the other, they're trying to encourage (and at the same time domesticate) the torrent of change brought on by the new economy. As a result, they're moving sideways, instead of straight ahead.

Government Adjustment

Governments have not yet adjusted much more than their rhetoric to the changed economic conditions they confront. On the contrary. They proved immensely reluctant to allow market forces to reassert themselves. It took authorities 10 years to realize that the best way to stabilize exchange rates was to ensure steady domestic prices. The need for real political independence from the government of the day, which credible monetary policy requires, was new territory to most central bankers. Governments usually continued to assert that they had the same control over their national economies as they did when currencies were shielded from daily capital movements. Governments still rose and fell on job creation, not price stability. The outcome of this mismatch between political goals and economic realities was a decade of inflation and economic stagnation, as well as escalating public debt as governments borrowed to maintain living standards, hoping in vain for a turnaround.

Voters seemed to understand the futility of this pattern of state behavior a decade ago, when they began electing governments that would redraw the boundaries of state economic intervention. In countries that stayed the course for the full supply-side treatment, as it was called, full employment and steady, non-inflationary growth is back. But the new jobs are different—they're not related to political programs, they're based on the needs of international companies. The working conditions are different—they're established through international competition, with less influence from trade union bargaining, and the pay scales are competitive. The overall result, full employment and non-inflationary growth, has been a reality for some 10 years now—something the welfare state promised, but was never able to deliver, after the reconstruction of Europe was completed in the mid-1960s.

The casualties in this development are the very institutions upon which millions of people nevertheless relied to maintain jobs: governments and trade unions. In most OECD countries, government employment has leveled off and union membership is declining where it's not mandated.

Spending Role Continues

Yet perhaps surprisingly, governments' spending role in the national economies of the West has not diminished. They still spend between 35 and 50 per cent of the total value of goods and services produced each year, despite privatizations and restructuring and de-regulation of state-controlled sectors. This is remarkable, considering that the post- Bretton-Woods era of floating rates has substantially reduced

Table 4.1 Total Government Spending (%GDP) 1980-96			
Country	1980	1990	1996
Canada	38.8	46.0	44.7
France	46.1	49.8	54.5
Germany	47.9	45.1	49.0
UK	43.0	39.9	41.9
US	31.4	32.8	33.5

Source: OECD in Figures, Public Sector, various years

government's ability to protect its work force from economic risk. The chart above shows this clearly. What *has* changed is governments' *pattern* of spending. From the 1960s onwards—with no slacking in the 70s and

80s, the supposedly supply-side period of national finance strategies—expenditures continued to grow along with GDP. In particular, spending increased on transfers to persons—to the unemployed, to the impoverished, and to the aged.

As program spending and support to state enterprises and state-delivered services has diminished, governments have focused even more tightly on redistributing income to individuals, within the constraints of low to zero deficits. The startling fact about government's responses is that they've managed to continue spending by raising taxes dramatically.

Governments can't borrow like they used to, because if they hadn't cleaned up their balance sheets by slashing deficits and paying down debt, global money markets would simply have bid up interest rates as a way of getting paid for assuming the extra risk of the additional borrowing. At a certain point, the costs of borrowing would have exceeded the returns the additional government spending was to be used for.

So governments turned to taxpayers, particularly those in the top income brackets, without sparing other taxpayers much either. The downloading of program costs from federal to provincial to municipal governments is one way the adjustment costs of government remain in the taxpayer's pocket; even though some taxes may go down (e.g. provincial or state income tax), others go up (such as municipal property taxes). While this waltz has shored up the balance sheets and allowed governments to proclaim they had their finances under control, it has avoided the deeper question: what services *should* government supply and how should they be paid for?

Reluctant as they may be to confront this question, governments must do so, because their current pattern of behavior can't be sustained. It represents an abject failure by government to reinvent itself in a form suitable to the age in which it finds itself. Perhaps even more ominously, it means that our political systems have been unable to adjust the way our economic systems have. The countries of the West are facing a major disconnect between the role of the state and the underlying economic reality.

In particular, the tax strategies are unsustainable, which is hazardous to the health of the global economy. Yet governments need a healthy global economy to fulfill the obligations they've already contracted, never mind any new ones. What *has* changed since globalization began to bite is that government tax strategies now impose higher indirect taxes (sales taxes, user fees, unemployment fund contributions and social security levies) on average and below-average income taxpayers, while increasing income taxes on above-average earners. In many OECD countries most taxpayers now pay more in sales taxes and service levies than they do in income tax. Yet in gross revenue terms, states remain heavily dependent on income taxes applied to the most mobile sectors of the population. The text box below sets out the main lines of the new taxation.

These public sector adjustment strategies are ultimately likely to be self-defeating. High taxes inhibit economic growth. Low growth induces higher unemployment and under-employment, which increases demand for income transfers via government. We saw the result in the mid-1970s and 80s: a self-destructive round of low growth; more state program spending; then higher taxes and/or deficits to pay for programs. Then higher interest rates as capital markets seek payment for the added risk of lending, then less employment and investment, and so on. This process amounts to a vicious circle that cripples the ability of states to extricate themselves from the problems looming ahead. Worse, unless governments bite the bullet on 'rightsizing'—undertaking significant reduction and reform by using information technology to facilitate current activity—some national governments may be tempted by this vicious tax circle to 'throw a spanner into the works' on trade. Bad as the prospects are for such a course, the costs of change are

huge. For example, the costs of equipping governments with the necessary information technology—any governments, but especially in middle-income and developing countries without high performance telecommunications networks—will be billions of dollars, even if the subsequent cost savings will be dramatic. Most governments don't have this money and are reluctant to weaken other programs in order to give money to IT suppliers. The political case for such investment may be worse if the money will flow out to a rich

---

The New Taxation

How sustainable is the national tax base, now that we've globalized our economies? Governments' ability to govern depends of their ability to tax. But one of the consequences of globalization is that more individuals and firms have more flexibility about where they pay taxes. Currently, it's precisely those who have acquired a new mobility who pay the most tax, because they are for the most part well-educated professionals and senior executives who command high incomes. National states are already becoming concerned about the continued viability of their tax base.

There are two kinds of national tax bases: 'mobile' and 'fixed.' Over the last 10 years, as globalization becomes more pervasive, states have been less able to tax such mobile items as profits and wealth, while taxes on labor,such as payroll and UI, and consumption taxes, such as sales taxes, value-added taxes, and user fees, are rising.These are fixed tax bases, because the tax is levied as the transactions occur.

One of the fastest-growing taxes in OECD countries is Social Security tax, which is a payroll deduction. At the same time, taxes have increased substantially in response to demands from money markets that governments bring receipts into line with spending and start paying down accumulated debt. In OECD Europe, the overall tax-to-GDP ratio increased from 27% to 40% in the early '90s. In five European countries—Belgium, Denmark, Finland, France and Sweden— the tax take in 1996 exceeded 45% of GDP. In Australia, Japan and New Zealand,the ratio climbed from 22% to 30 % of GDP. Only in North America, where tax cuts in the US balanced tax increases in Canada, has it remained relatively constant, at around 25% of GDP.

Taxes on personal and corporate incomes are the main revenue sources of 14 OECD countries and in five of them—Australia, Canada, Denmark, New Zealand and the United States—they make up a revenue share in excess of 45% of the total. These countries are especially vulnerable in the light of the future demand for senior, experienced corporate executives, forecast to be in critically short supply early in the 21st century.) The war for talent is so intense, countries that try to get most of their revenue from such people are probably doomed to find themselves with fewer of them, and therefore lower levels of prosperity.

Direct taxes are unlikely to make up the shortfall. Before World War I, when 63% of government revenue came from property taxes, it amounted to less than 6% of GDP. There's a limit to the usefulness of direct taxes. Higher taxes on labor just slow job creation and stimulate the operation of illegal labor markets. Continued pursuit of this track will simply worsen the problem.

1

foreign country. But the alternatives are worse still. For example, if unemployment rises in countries unwilling or unable to adjust quickly enough, they may return to protectionism to create jobs. It doesn't take much imagination to see the world reversing the trade liberalization that has been so crucial to the unprecedented wealth creation of the past 50 years.

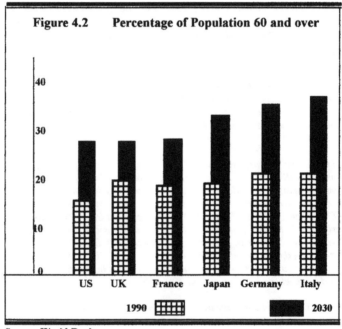

Figure 4.2 Percentage of Population 60 and over

Source: World Bank

Demographic Impact

The second problem is the impact of demographics on government-supplied services. These services were established on a pay-as-you-go basis when it seemed that each generation would be more plentiful than the last. However, this was not to be. States now face a double whammy, from demographics and the impact of globalization on taxation that makes adjustment inevitable. The text box below summarizes the main concerns.

Here's what the demographics mean for the wealth-generating capacity of countries over the next decades: falling employment as a share of total population, and decreasing ability to pay down the financial liabilities governments have accumulated. (These are set out in Figures 4.2 and 4.3.)

The aging of Canada's work force follows international trends, although Canada's population remains a bit younger than that of the other G-7 economies. Between 1996 and 2006, the population aged 45 and up increases significantly faster than all other age groups combined. Indeed every 10-year interval (45-55, 55-65) above age 45 increases faster than any cohort under age 45. As a result of these demographic trends, labor force participation in Canada will peak at 65 per cent in 2001 and decline to 59 per cent by 2021.[xxv] As for productivity, Canada's productivity growth, while increasing, is lagging that of the US and even the OECD average, which means that even with a growing work force, Canadian living standards are deteriorating relative to its major economic partners.[xxvi] Even the most optimistic picture of Canada's outlook shows that for the country to be able to meet its obligations to the boomers without a tax hike, the government will have to continue to accumulate surpluses on the order of 3.5 per cent of GDP *for the next 30 years*.[xxvii]

In Canada's trillion-dollar (C$) economy, that amounts to a surplus of $3.5 billion each year, compounded by the annual growth rate, which is itself around 2 to 4 per cent a year. Although it may not sound like much, a government revenue surplus that each year matches or exceeds economic growth is predatory and destructive in its effect on business investment decisions, by far the most important source of economic growth in a country whose population is not growing rapidly. A moment's reflection will make this clear:

why invest to achieve added output if you know that most additional output will be eaten up in taxes? As we've emphasized, the new technologies enhance the mobility of investment capital and allow individual business persons to allocate tax revenue to other countries, i.e. (in this case) outside Canada. What these considerations mean, more generally, is that programs based on the tax-and-spend assumptions of the past will fail whenever they threaten individual living standards.

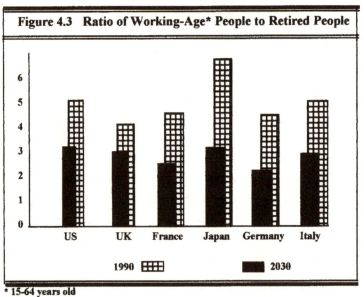

Figure 4.3   Ratio of Working-Age* People to Retired People

* 15-64 years old
Source: World Bank, ILO

Nor does the optimistic scenario take into account the spillover effects of other governments' defaults on Canada's own capital market picture. Tax hikes by the Europeans and Americans that dampened economic growth would lower Canadian growth and reduce the revenue flows to Ottawa. A debt scramble by the EU and the US to borrow enough money to finance its aging boomers could easily raise rates enough to slash Canada's economic growth rates. The possibility of a fiscal black hole is very real if governments don't face up to the new reality and redesign not only these programs but the way they do business in general. Finally, the technology revolution we're living through virtually ensures that taxpayers will be able to decide whether to continue to direct their money to government programs they don't believe in or to private investments that they do. Indeed, allowing such choices to occur easily would make more sense than continuing to deny the situation now staring welfare-state treasuries in the face.

Governments, according to the OECD, have a limited amount of time to deal with this issue. Their 1999 wake-up call reads as follows:

> The main demographic changes start to come in 10 or 15 years' time. This gives our societies a limited window of opportunity in which to introduce reforms in areas such as pensions and other social programmes, financial markets, health and long-term care. Advance action is desirable on several counts.

> Some reforms will affect future retirees, who have few means of adjusting once they are retired, and advance announcement of reforms, together with clear timetables for phasing them in, gives them time to adjust in an optimal manner while they are still of working age. Those adjustments in themselves will likely reduce eventual fiscal and social strains.

> Second, if reforms are delayed until the demographic pressures dictate them, they will have to be all the more severe, and risk either distorting labour markets to an unacceptable degree, or sparking off a renewed period of climbing public sector deficits and debt, thus undoing all the hard won gains of the recent past. It would, for example, be much easier to manage the new fiscal pressures from a position of fiscal surpluses.

Demographics

The World War II generation that established the welfare state is its chief beneficiary in terms of retirement programs. It based the funding of those programs on the assumption that populations would continue to expand. There would always be more workers to carry the retirement burden of the preceding generation. Intergenerational transfers, (i.e. obligations incurred by one generation on behalf of another) are generally avoided in public policy on ethical grounds, but the burden of supporting one's parents was generally the only alternative available to most people. If this burden were spread through the tax system ,more people would be better off. As to the ethics, such programs were only an extension of private ethics to the public sphere. The problem is that the children of the World War II generation have NOT had more children—they've had the same number or fewer.

Consequently, the population graphs that used to look like pyramids (lots of young people at the base, with only a few seniors at the top) now look like lemons. Ahead of the boomers, a decreasing group of the war vets generations; then the bulge of their kids, the boomers; after the boomers (and an 'echo' from their kids), fewer children. This demographic fact undermines the original assumption behind pensions and health-care maintenance of the present generation. The ratio between workers and tax-supported non-workers was expected to go down over time: in fact that ratio is going up.

The other demographic problem is that older people are living much longer. Today's fastest-growing age group is between 65 and 100. Indeed, the chances are if you make it to retirement at 65, you'll probably live at least another 20 years. Somehow, the current generation of workers must therefore finance its own family while simultaneously paying millions of otherwise reasonably healthy 70-year-olds to stay out of the work force.

The upshot is that the pension and health care promises made by the government cannot now be funded without either (a) a massive hike in taxes, or (b) a significant reduction in benefits. There is, of course, a middle ground, in which programs would be re-thought in line with other changes that are taking place in society. Our concepts of retirement could be adjusted, as have our concepts of work. Governments know this. But, as The Economist *pointed out as long ago as June 1998, they've been astonishingly reluctant to discuss changes.*

Further, clear goals and timetables would help build support for sustained reform. The need for reform is understood in general terms. For example, many younger people do not now believe that decent public pensions will still be available when they retire. However there is less understanding of the solutions such as working later, that will be needed.

Source: Maintaining Prosperity in an Ageing Society, OECD, 1998, p.34

Without a change in programs, solvency in the major European countries requires an increased contribution rate of 20 per cent. More important, net government debt will increase by 100 per cent in Europe and Japan. In North America, that rate of increase is much less for the pension account—a 20 per cent increase in net debt in the US, which can be covered by contribution increases of just six per cent from 1992 levels. The bottom line is that pensions, and with pensions the whole social contract, must be changed, especially in Europe.[xxviii]

Yet there is one way out, which the authors of the OECD report did not discuss: increased productivity—especially the increased productivity that can come from the new economy. For the system to stave off depression, productivity has to increase at least sufficiently to make up for the fall in productive labor. That is, as the labor force falls from a peak of around 50 per cent of the population to a trough of less than 40 per cent, productivity must make up the output gap left by the missing workers—a gap of 10-15 per cent over 20 years or more. Is such a productivity increase feasible? Other data suggest that it is. Bear in mind that productivity measurement is difficult even in one country. International inconsistencies complicate output comparisons: the issues of foreign exchange conversion, different taxes imposed at different points in the value chain, etc. But the general trends in leading OECD countries over the 20 years between 1975 and 1995 [xxix]—that is, during the weakening of the welfare state and the rise of globalization — are encouraging. The most productive country in terms of manufacturing output per hour is the US. It achieved an impressive 10 per cent rate of increase over the period after 1980. Equally encouraging, so did many other countries.

Data analyzed by other researchers tell a similar story. The US leads in manufacturing labor productivity, but the rate of increase over the 20-year period of economic liberalization and globalization has been equally positive for most leading countries.[xxx] (Canada has not kept pace with US productivity growth in recent years, making its retirement dilemma particularly acute.[xxxi])

Productivity is essentially the responsibility of the private sector. Governments can help by having good legal structures, encouraging education and maintaining non-inflationary price levels. But productivity growth occurs when more productive activities and firms replace less productive ones. Productivity is a by-product of competition and innovation. Firms up-size and down-size to become more productive: the efficient scale of enterprise depends in part on the maturity of the industry. Regulation generally favors the incumbent. Deregulation that keeps incumbent power in check and encourages competition also encourages productivity gains. Liberalizing trade rules to improve competition has the same effect. The process of liberalization and deregulation over the last 20 years laid the foundations for the new economy that is generating the productivity gains the world needs to overcome the burden of an aging workforce. More globalization, more innovation and more economic dynamism are essential to safeguard that prosperity.

With continued productivity growth, OECD economies could maintain levels of prosperity and meet required levels of support to an aging population. But there is a caveat—it can only happen if liberalization, globalization and the shift to the new economy continue to accelerate.

Thus, governments have to redesign themselves appropriately. They have to rethink themselves and what they do, and they have to do it in time to permit these levels of productivity growth to continue. Otherwise, the long boom will end as growth bumps up against impediments, living standards will no longer continue to rise, and any governments that are still around will probably default on their massive obligations. This could plunge the world into deep recession or decades of stagnation (as in Japan, currently). We might very well see the transformation of today's virtuous circles of growth-generated positive feedback into vicious circles of negative feedback that hobble recovery for many years.

In effect, governments are caught in the following paradox: to live up to the contracts they've written, they have to embrace the new economy, but doing so will dramatically change the government and, in all likelihood, the contracts too.

"It Won't Happen!"

Unlike the private sector, which has adapted to a global information age, governments are continuing to play by the old rules of industrial society. Instead of seriously redesigning themselves, they are focusing on re-aligning old forms of regulation. Instead of reforming the tax system, they are making tax systems even more invasive. Instead of stepping aside, governments are trying to maintain their primacy of place and to continue making policy as if nothing fundamental has changed. Governments have been very slow to admit that there are limits to their competence—they still act as if they can solve every problem. But politics is not just a contest about redistribution in which economists argue with each other about growth rates, productivity and taxes. And governments haven't done the hard work of re-thinking what they should be doing now and in the future. That discussion is an ethical discussion and it's now being led by the new, cyber-linked civil society—not governments.

Fundamentally, the states of the West have resisted restructuring themselves from what they have been since World War II. Despite the changes that have trashed the assumptions underlying their structure and performance, the executive and legislative branches of today's leading governments remain firmly unmodified in every important respect. In defiance of information-age politics, they are still made up of huge departments managed by vertical authority stacks and run on the myth that all power comes from the top. Thus, they are set up as a vertically arranged group of people with a deputy minister or secretary or director at the top and cascading authority down to the analyst who actually works on the file. Today, that analyst could probably do it all with the information available to anyone with a modem, a computer and a small research budget, and hand the data directly to the politician for decision. But in state structures today, information that might take an individual a couple of hours to develop takes a department days, weeks, months—depending on its urgency and how controversial it is.

That's because analysts still have to pass information up and down the vertical authority chain before they can decide what to do with it. Then there's the challenge of enlisting cross-departmental support. This is even more difficult to achieve: coupled with the needs of authority are the procedures of budgeting. Vertical departments remain at the heart of every national budget process. Hence any attempt to re-arrange governments more horizontally raises the specter of a loss of departmental budget resources. Not surprisingly, in some countries the bureaucracy is actively thwarting attempts to wire government, for that reason.

How else might governments operate? What adjustments would be reasonable to expect them to carry out? The list below recaps some guidelines for the US federal government's re-organization to provide 'digital government.' A similar table can be constructed from a more recent OECD publication, *Government of the Future*.

We would go further to say that digitizing government will make *results* as important as *process* and *transparency* because of the new importance of competence as a legitimizer of public policy. It's perhaps a measure of bureaucratic power in countries today that nearly all government spending is directly related to process rather than outcomes. School spending will increase, or computers will be supplied. But left unstated is what we mean by education, what performance leader we should benchmark against and what the measurable outcomes will be. To be sure, when things actually matter, governments sometimes do talk this way; budgets are useful documents for the financial community because they set out the extent to which governments will borrow. That's an end in itself for a bond dealer. But what about the rest of us?

PRINCIPLES FOR IMPLEMENTING DIGITAL GOVERNMENT

1. Think Customer, not Government Agency
2. Reinvent Government, Don't Simply Automate It
3. Set an Ambitious Goal
4. Invest Now to Save Tomorrow
5. Focus on Digital Transactions Between Citizens and Government
6. Make Government Applications Interoperable with Commercial Ones
7. Pass on a Portion of Savings from Electronic Transactions Back to Citizens
8. Promote Access to Information on the Internet. Do Not Restrict It.
9. Respect the Rights of Americans for Information Privacy
10. Online Access to Government Should Not Eclipse Traditional Means
11. Federal Efforts Should Complement, Not Duplicate Private Sector Efforts
12. Take Action Now, and Learn From Mistakes

Source: Robert D. Atkinson and Jacob Ulevich, *Digital Government: The Next Step to Re- Engineering the Federal Government*, Progressive Policy Institute, Technology and New Economy Project, March 2000, p.10 (available on-line at www.dlcppi.org)

If governments wanted to define educational outcomes and then help society attain them, it is also obvious that they are not competent to do this themselves. They would have to establish some kind of national decision-making process on this and the program would involve more interests than government alone. Nor would it be enough to throw together some blue-ribbon panels and hear from interest groups. This happens already, and results are generally disappointing. Information-age governments could go beyond this, but a lot would have to change along the way.

Not only governments, but citizens, too, would have to change. Essentially, we would have to alter our notions of what it means to be a citizen and our expectations of government. We would have to be a lot more willing to cooperate in supplying our own public services to ourselves. But then we could enlist the aid of government, as a partner with some identifiable competencies, perhaps in the area of goal articulation and resource mobilization. While there is not much on the horizon to provide immediate encouragement, there are some hopeful signs at least that the present set-up cannot long continue. The collapsing tax base of the welfare state is the death knell of this regime.

If this seems a dire consequence, perhaps it should be remembered that a weakened ability to tax is a common precursor of a change in the format of the state. It was the failing tax base of the *ancien régime* that fatally undermined its claim to competence, just as the Depression destroyed the belief in the long-term stability of market forces. In the current conjuncture of economic, political and technological forces, the welfare state as we've come to know it—that is, the state built on tax and transfer programs—is scarcely viable. The historical pattern of such changes is clear. More difficult are the adjustments required to manage change on the scale required.

#

PART TWO

Changing the Nature of the State

Chapter 5

Does Territory Still Matter?

"Governments of the industrial world, you weary giant of flesh and steel. You have no sovereignty where we gather."
—Jon Perry Barlow, A Cyberspace Independence Declaration

Two hundred years ago, at the dawn of the modern nation state, James Madison observed in the Federalist Papers on the General Power of Taxation that

> Money is…considered as the vital principle of the body politic; as that which sustains its life and motion, and enables it to perform its essential functions. From a deficiency in this particular, one of two evils must ensue: either the people must be subjected to continual plunder, as a substitute for a more eligible mode of supplying the public wants, or the government must sink into a fatal atrophy, and, in a short course of time, perish.

If the Net is making business even more competitive, it is also posing problems for tax collectors. The fundamental problem is that governments are linked to physical space whereas the Internet has no spatial dimension. Transactions on the Net occur in time, but not in space. This fact has not been lost on national and regional revenue departments. State governors in the US, for example, claim that the trend to cyberspace is costing them billions in lost sales taxes. They are concerned that the trend will impose a bigger tax burden on those who are less intensive in their Net applications. At the national level, the US has begun to fear the tax evasive power of e-commerce.[xxxii] But at whatever level you like, the question remains: where will the authorities apply the tax when jurisdictions are territorial and the Net is not?

Taxation and De-territorialization

Efficient revenue-raising taxes should be behavior-neutral. In other words, an efficient tax should not induce the taxpayer to change his, hers or its affairs to avoid the tax. An efficient tax should be non-discriminatory: that is, it should fall upon all those who are liable to pay it. In practical terms, an efficient tax has as broad a base as possible, consistent with non-discrimination and behavior neutrality. Nor should compliance impose an intolerable burden on those who fall within the definition of 'liable.'

It's not easy to see how these conditions can be met with a Net tax of any kind. The flexibility and adaptability of the Net suggests that behavior-neutrality would be impossible to achieve. The worldwide nature of the Web indicates that the incidence of any national tax would always be discriminatory. The sheer complexity of adjusting tax rates between locations of suppliers and customers also suggests that compliance would be excessively burdensome, although software could be devised to enable sellers to collect taxes from buyers according to 1) location of the seller, and 2) location of the buyer. Some proposals for a net tax seek to use the commercial power of major markets, such as the US or the EU, as certifiers. That is, to qualify for a particular standing (such as a financial intermediary) in those lucrative markets, an enterprise would have to register, comply with certain reporting rules, etc. Such an approach, quasi-voluntary, bottom-up, may have a better chance of adoption than a sales tax. However, all these approaches overlook the question of the sheer volume of Net traffic and the cost-effectiveness of policing it in any meaningful way.

In some ways, the fight over Net taxes represents a clash of cultural values reminiscent of the clashes over native land when Europeans first came to North America. For Europeans, land was valuable space that could be owned. The native North Americans had no concept of land ownership and saw territory in terms of the time it took to cross. For example, Amerindian natives drew maps that showed the passage of time rather than space. A famous voyageur map shows the Great Lakes displayed on a scale that indicated the time necessary to pass different sections of the route. Since large lakes were relatively easy to cross in heavily laden canoes compared to streams and the portages between them, the 'time' map seemed the reverse of fact when interpreted in spatial terms: small streams loomed large, while the Great Lakes were represented as much smaller. Similarly in industrial societies, money is a concept inseparable from the *physical* instruments of money—cash, gold, certificates, etc. In the idea economy, money is simply more bits and bytes of information—about quantity, time, risk—all the factors that affect the *value* of money. But the *physical* presence of money is not very interesting—in fact, it's a hindrance because you can't do anything with cash in cyberspace. It has to be in bits.

The clash over Net taxation is not just about sums of money. It's also an example of the kind of struggle that shows up when whole cultures come under pressure as technologies change. Governments are focused on funds in the form of money—the actual tokens—not as information. They can be forgiven for a traditional focus because they operate in physical space with physical objects as they always have. But this is beside the point in an information age.

Look at it this way. Money has to be transported in physical space and thus can always be stolen or lost—or taxed. Money also depends on its exclusivity-of-ownership properties to maintain its value. In contrast, information is persistent, has no physical presence, and depends on time for its value.

The issue is not exclusivity but rather *when* the information is shared and what recipients already know. An efficient information tax would therefore have to delay/accelerate the flow of information in return for value. Space is irrelevant. If I could transact faster by paying a tax than not paying it, I would pay the tax. Otherwise, forget it. (This is the theory behind 'Quality of Service' pricing for Internet service, in which a premium price would guarantee top service with no delays, no information loss, etc.)

So far, the Internet tax debate is mainly about how physical transactions handled through the Net can be translated into tax records in the customer's jurisdiction. The issue is whether the customer was in that jurisdiction when the transaction took place and whether the product bought was in the same legal territory as the server recording the transaction. It's an attempt to translate an act in physical space into an act in cyberspace— and the translation won't work very well because the underlying structure of transactions in cyberspace is different: there is no "place", there is only "when". Transactions exist in time, not space.

In a similar way, tax authorities are helpless before another phenomenon of cyberspace, the new wealth available on the Net as a result of cooperative activity. This new wealth of information is posted to help people add to their individual understanding of the world or to empower them to play an effective role in public debates and social action campaigns. The taxman's view of the Net thus understates its value as a social tool and ignores its potential significance as a means of reducing state involvement in social issues, and state spending in particular.

One upshot of the state's focus on money as the international economy moves to the Net is that it (ironically) makes taxation much more voluntary. For example, I might decide to make the social contribution the tax is designed to cover, but I no longer feel compelled to do so. I could organize my affairs to get around the tax, but I would be prepared to make the tax payment if I benefited by some amount equal or superior to that which the tax demands. In such a case I'd be paying voluntarily, just as I may voluntarily pay user fees of various kinds, such as road taxes, tolls, parks, snow removal, maybe even fees for education and day-care facilities if I have young children.

An important conclusion to draw from all this is that in the information age, governments have to sell services even to those nominally paying taxes; they can't continue to just collect taxes by coercive means. As to a tax that would affect information flows, such a tax is not feasible in the Net's architecture: the Net was expressly designed to keep information flowing, no matter what. As more and more economic activity moves to the Net, the state will be left relying on fixed sources of revenue, as in the 19th century: land tax, head taxes, and fees for government services. Taxpayers may be prepared to pay taxes voluntarily, but only for services they feel are valuable. OECD tax guidelines try to avoid the spatial problem by defining "physical presence" as the basis of direct tax liability in a particular jurisdiction. A server may double as "physical presence"—a web page does not. In so doing, these guidelines seek to avoid the main effects of the shift to e-commerce, wealth will continue to be taxed where it is created—but it can be created any place the taxpayer wants to create it.[xxxiii]

Self-organizing Territoriality: The Tiebout Model

Governments are about territory. Industrial society, like the agricultural society before it, was rooted in land. People worked specific pieces of land. Then they worked in factories at specific locations. In old economic models, people didn't move. When land became unproductive or the economy tanked in one region, national governments set the rules for the rest of the country to help. But now people also migrate. Within countries—absent other considerations—people in industrial societies are not tied to land and can move freely. In modern national economies, people can move to jobs—and in global, electronically linked information economies, people can work anywhere someone will hire them.

The reasons people move, and the barriers established by one group to prevent others from migrating, have been subjects of study for years. The migration to the suburbs in the 1940s and 50s supplied data from which economists have refined their models of in-country migration. In particular, American economist Charles Tiebout theorized in the mid-1950s that when local governments provide public goods, taxpayers will organize themselves so that where they live matches their preferences for taxes and services. Those that like higher quality services and are prepared to pay for them will move to those neighborhoods. Those with different preferences will align themselves accordingly. The value of neighborhoods can be enhanced by a decision to provide better quality services. His model describes what is called 'jurisdiction shopping;' it includes the tax- shopping behavior that the Internet has opened up to more individuals, and adds the search for appropriate levels of public services. The encouraging thing for governments about this model is that it's not a one-way street: people shop up-market as well as down.

The Tiebout model demonstrates an important principle—people have the right to shop jurisdictions in order to ensure that taxes paid equal benefits received. The theory of voluntary taxation holds that the taxpayer at the mid-range of income should receive as much tax benefit as she pays in taxation, while those below middle income receive more and those above pay more. The equality of income distribution shored up by the tax system, so the theory goes, adds to economic stability. There is also a political argument, more prevalent in the 1940s and 50s when memories of Depression and war and fears of Communist alternatives were all top of mind. Progressive taxation ensures that those whom the market disadvantages will continue to benefit from the political system—this in turn lends stability to the system to encourage investment and economic growth.

Tiebout's model takes the voluntary tax theory further: taxpayers at all levels have the right and the capacity to seek out an appropriate mix of tax-paid services. That way, taxes paid and services received can equalize at the level of the household. Although originally designed to explain the mix of taxes and services in what were then-emerging suburbs at the edge of big cities, the Tiebout model also points to the way public finance may work once the commercial and civil society presence on the Net achieves critical mass. Entrepreneurs and workers in cyberspace will also be able to shop jurisdictions without leaving home. How? By taking advantage of the tax treaties that globalization requires if companies are to be able to operate interdependent production anywhere on the planet.

To facilitate economic growth, firms require access to large markets, as we have already seen. For most countries, this means a heavy dependence on international markets and with that, a tax system that avoids double counting. In other words, money already taxed in one jurisdiction must be exempt from taxation in the others. This principle is at the basis of tax treaties between governments. Even before firms organized themselves in networks, those that were doing business across borders had already worked out a number of techniques to ensure that they were able to take their tax burden in the jurisdictions they prefer.

Foreign Tax Credits

Most domestic tax systems give those with world-wide income sources the choice of where to pay taxes. As globalization advances, the number of tax treaties between states has multiplied. These treaties allow taxes paid in one country to be offset against taxes owing in another through a system of foreign tax credits. As more companies develop international connections because of the distribution of their value chains, the more it is possible for the owners and managers to organize their revenue accordingly. Total tax paid remains the same, but the taxpayer can allocate the location of the payments.

Business Taxes v. Individual Taxes

Today, small business owners have the choice of being taxed as a business or as an individual. Taxes on individuals have risen on average 45% in the OECD countries in the last 10 years, while taxes on corporations have diminished sharply. The table below shows the proportions of taxes paid by individuals and companies in OECD countries in 1995. Since then, corporation taxes have dropped in some countries. There are advantages to paying at the corporate or small business rate rather than at the individual rate. Increasingly, individuals are setting up small businesses to take advantage of the relatively more generous tax climate they have. Most jurisdictions also allow people to split income from a business with family members, even children, so that the tax they pay is usually at lower rates than those on a high-income individual. The Internet makes it easier to offer business services at low cost: many people have converted hobbies into profitable sidelines. Many others have converted hobbies into attractive tax shelters.

Going International

International operations are relatively easy to establish today; it is possible to reduce individual tax still more. Business owners pay taxes in whatever business jurisdiction they like, according to their preferences for booking income. International managers and high-powered consultants have been able to do this for years. The power of the Internet is that it gives all commercially active Internet participants the same power that global company managers have had for years, namely to enjoy a more truly voluntary tax system.

Another option open to the internationally connected is the ability to accumulate wealth in offshore bank accounts in tax-free havens, such as the Bahamas, the Dutch Antilles, and some European jurisdictions. This privilege is currently an elite rather than a mass activity. But Internet banking—on-line banks with no physical presence outside the tax shelter host country—would make it possible for everyone to do this. With the ability of ordinary individuals to conduct on-line purchases from such accounts, the cost to states of tracking offshore income will become extremely expensive, to the point where the cost of the tracking exceeds the tax benefits. Moreover, if the on-line purse were maintained in a basket of currencies with instructions to spend the weakest first and receive payments in the strongest, the dangers of international currency fluctuations would be sharply reduced.

As this book nears completion, the OECD is trying to bring pressure on countries whose banking laws still respect depositor privacy. Even if these efforts are successful, the fact of global life remains: people will still be able to allocate income according to value received.[i]

Table 5.1					Taxation						
				Tax structures as a percentage of total tax receipts							
Country	Total Tax Receipts, % of GDP	Personal Income Tax	Corporate Income Tax	Social Security Contributions Employees	Social Security Contributions Employers	Taxes on goods and services	Other taxes	Highest personal income tax rate	Lowest personal income tax rate	Disposable Income of average production worker as % of gross pay Single	Disposable Income of average production worker as % of gross pay Married, 2 children
Australia	30.7	40.6	14.7	0.0	0.0	29.2	15.5	47.0	36.0	76.0	83.9
Austria	42.4	20.9	3.7	15.7	17.5	27.7	14.6	50.0	34.0	73.0	90.5
Belgium	46.5	31.5	6.7	10.9	20.1	25.9	4.9	60.5	40.2	58.9	80.5
Canada	37.2	37.3	8.1	5.4	11.1	25.5	12.6	54.2	43.1	72.9	83.4
Czech Rep.	44.3	12.4	12.3	9.7	26.4	33.1	6.2	40.0	39.0	76.8	96.7
Denmark	51.3	53.7	4.1	2.5	0.6	32.4	6.6	60.0	34.0	54.3	69.1
Finland	46.5	34.8	5.3	4.4	22.1	29.7	3.7	62.1	26.0	62.0	73.7
France	44.5	13.9	3.7	13.1	26.8	27.3	15.2	56.9	33.3	72.6	85.2
Germany	39.2	27.3	2.8	17.1	20.0	27.8	5.1	57.0	45.3	59.5	75.0
Greece	41.4	11.8	6.2	15.8	14.4	40.5	11.2	57.0	40.3	82.4	82.9
Hungary	39.2	16.7	4.9	6.2	20.5	44.9	6.9	40.0	18.0	72.1	92.7
Iceland	31.2	31.1	3.	0.3	7.8	48.8	9.0	42.0	33.0	79.4	114.5*
Ireland	33.0	30.7	8.5	4.6	8.9	40.7	6.5	46.3	38.0	70.8	82.1
Italy	41.3	26.2	8.7	6.7	20.9	27.3	10.3	48.0	52.2	72.5	80.4
Japan	20.5	21.4	15.2	14.4	18.3	15.1	15.5	67.2	37.5	86.6	91.4
Korea	22.3	16.9	12.2	2.9	5.1	42.6	18.3	66.0	31.1	95.2	95.2
Luxembourg	44.0	21.3	17.5	10.7	12.3	27.1	11.0	44.5	39.0	74.4	98.8
Mexico	16.0	–	–	–	–	55.7	–	50.0	34.0	89.5	89.5
Netherlands	44.0	18.9	7.5	27.1	6.7	27.4	12.4	60.0	35.0	59.5	70.2
Norway	41.5	44.2	12.0	0.0	0.0	33.3	10.5	33.0	33.0	75.5	77.6
Poland	42.7	22.9	7.7	0.0	30.4	35.2	3.7	44.0	38.0	81.9	89.9
Portugal	33.8	18.0	8.0	10.1	15.4	43.5	4.9	40.0	39.6	82.0	90.8
Spain	34.0	23.8	5.5	6.3	25.0	29.7	10.8	56.0	35.0	80.4	87.2
Sweden	49.7	36.3	6.1	3.6	24.9	24.3	5.8	60.6	28.0	67.4	76.2
Switzerland	33.9	31.5	5.7	12.0	11.5	18.5	20.8	43.9	39.8	77.5	90.5
Turkey	22.5	21.6	6.7	4.7	6.3	37.6	23.1	55.0	25.0	69.6	69.6
UK	35.3	27.4	9.5	7.4	9.6	34.7	11.4	40.0	33.0	73.3	81.4
US	27.9	36.3	9.4	10.7	13.1	17.9	12.5	46.6	39.6	74.2	81.4
EU Average	41.8	26.4	5.9	10.4	16.3	31.0	9.0	53.9	36.3	69.6	81.7
OECD Avg.	37.4	27.0	8.0	8.0	14.1	32.4	10.4	49.9	35.1	73.8	85.1

Source: Revenue Statistics, 1995-96, OECD, Paris, 1997 * Because benefits exceed taxes due, disposable income is higher than gross pay.

Say, for the sake of simplicity, Canadian and American currencies were of equal value and personal income taxes in Canada are twice those of the US. Therefore you can earn twice as much from US sources before owing the same amount of tax to the US as you would to Canadian authorities. Total taxes on, say, $100,000 in Canada would be $50,000, in the US, $25,000.

Relative to *domestic* competition, the foreign tax credit system benefits those in the higher tax country the most. For example, if you earned $100,000 income in Canada, you would keep $50,000 and send $50,000 to the national or provincial government (or both).

But if, as a Canadian resident, you earned half your income in the US, you would still owe $50,000 in tax on your worldwide income of $100,000. But you would already have paid $12,500 in US taxes on the US portion. So now you can claim from Canadian authorities the $12,500 in tax paid on the US portion of your income. Thus you would pay only $37,500 in Canadian tax, and would net $62,500 in Canada instead of $50,000. You still paid $50,000 in total tax, but by spreading it over two countries, you were able to pay less tax in the high tax country. The low tax country, perhaps surprisingly, gets an addition to its tax base, proving (as we explore further in Chapter 9) that in a global economy, less is more.

Even now, taxation systems leave some choice for individuals to adjust the level of taxes they pay to what they think is fair. In the future, however, this capability is bound to broaden significantly. The power of sovereign states to collect taxes is eroding: voluntary taxation, once only a theoretical proposition, is now within the grasp of a lot more commercially active people.

The Dual Culture of the Net

Governments' problems with taxing the Net are more than an issue of technology. Like governments' obsession with money, the wish to tax on-line transactions somehow sidesteps the large non-transactional nature of the

Net and Net culture. Like a community with a strong common spirit, there is also a part of the Net that involves co-operation as well as competition.

In all great cities, there's a feeling that goes beyond individual reciprocity: there's a sense of community. The Net, too, embodies a dual logic that is even more basic than e-commerce; embedded in the fundamental architecture of the Internet is a technology that enables people to work together in pursuit of common aims. In fact, its original 1940s architecture is that of collaboration and cooperation in pursuit of collective goals. The Net is a culture based on community values in contrast to individual transactional values.

Economists and other social scientists have long understood the selfish (in the jargon, 'individual maximizing') behavior of people engaged in commerce, but have struggled to explain the phenomenon of people cooperating for general benefit. Adam Smith wrote that it was in the nature of man to "barter, truck and trade", just as it was in human nature to be ruled by moral values. Anthropologists, animal behavior specialists, and economists have now determined that cooperative action is not only a fundamental condition of successful evolution, but is also as advantage-seeking as trying to get the most for the least. The ability to work together is at least as important as efficient prices in determining human survival. The inducements for human generosity can be as selfish as prestige, glory, or sexual opportunities. Giving to others can create obligation—the rational need to ensure that the effort one makes today will be reciprocated when one needs help at a later date. The table below explores the two Net cultures: the collaborative gift culture and the commercial, transactional culture. The table sets out some of the dimensions of competition between the transaction culture of physical space (reflected in the current dominant hardware for the Internet) and the competing values of the gift culture.

The gift culture is older than the transaction culture. It is the earliest group value, and obliges those who take something from the group to return something to it. It can reward those who give with added prestige.

(One variation of the gift culture was the potlatch tradition of the Pacific Northwest, in which prestige and social status were earned through the donation of immense wealth to the group. In the potlatch culture, such giving reinforced hierarchy; the Net culture is a great leveler.)

Table 5.2 The Collaborative and Commercial Net Cultures	
Collaborative (Gift)	**Commercial (Transactional)**
Based on reciprocity	Based on money
Information sharing	Information selling
Conversation	Pay-per-view
Shareware	Software sales
Interactive gaming	Multiplayer
Evolving software	Upgradeable software
Collaborative work	Work for hire
Donations community	Taxing community

The commercial, competitive model of Internet use has come late in the evolution of cyberspace, 50 years after the Net's designers created it as a fail-safe way for scientists and academics to communicate in an uncertain world. Although it is enjoying enormous success, it is also facing significant resistance through the development of collaboratively produced products with the potential to outperform the mass-produced, shrink-wrapped variety. In terms of practical activities, the two approaches are embodied in the emerging struggle between methods of

producing software. Should software be produced for sale, by a commercial enterprise, or should the users develop it free on an open source
basis? (That is, on a co-operative basis that makes the source code freely
available with the sole requirement that any user's modifications and
improvements be accessible to the other users of that software, wherever
they are.) The current struggle between Microsoft's Windows operating
system and the Linux emulator of Microsoft Windows is a dramatic
illustration of the conflict between the two approaches.

The Microsoft Windows system, which now covers 95 per cent of the
Net's screens, comes out of a box and is one-size-fits-all standardized. In
contrast, the Linux system is being designed and improved continually by
its users, and is free for the downloading. Proponents of the open source
approach claim that user-designed software outperforms anything possible
from a single private source. Therefore, as the Internet embraces more
advanced capabilities, user groups, not companies, will increasingly supply
those capabilities. Open source proponents believe that the translation of
industry-style intellectual property rights to the Net will fail, because they
are too restrictive to permit the continual evolution great software
requires. They also argue that such rules are unenforceable in a digitized
environment. Another type of group sharing behavior—the on-line swap-
meet currently incarnated in Napster and Gnutella (to name but two)
technologies—is changing the commercial environment for commercial
music. The specific case of Napster is being litigated as we write. But the
general point for purposes of our argument is this: what amounts to a
legitimate individual transaction—swapping already-paid-for songs for
personal use—becomes a serious challenge to conventional physical-
space-based business models when aggregated in cyberspace. The argument of this book can be boiled down to the simple proposition that
Napster-type activity is the future face of public life and policy.

Particularly interesting is how the 'make it free' group looks at human
behavior. What drives human creativity, they argue, is the condition of

being human. The Net, which has the potential to put everyone on the planet in touch with everyone else, will, by the very creation of this interactive context, touch off a creativity drive. The results will blow away the restrictive intellectual property rights that those who see the Net as a mainly transactional medium want to impose.

The Hacker Phenomenon

The Net's two cultures—the Gift relationship and the transactional culture overlaying it—coexist peacefully most of the time. But the different values ensure that a certain dark rivalry is also at work. The most potent sign of this is the hacker. 'Hacker' is the name given to someone who's technically adept and an ingenious problem solver. But the term has also come to be applied to those who use technical means to gain unauthorized access to protected files on the Net, sometimes inserting programs that will harm the data or the system's software.

In the last year, hundreds of thousands of credit card numbers were copied from an on-line music retailer. Melissa, an e-mail virus, went around the world causing an estimated $80 million worth of damage. Millions of calling card numbers were copied from AT&T, GTE and Sprint. Early in 2000 'denial of service' (DOS) attacks took down some of the Web's biggest and most technically proficient Web sites: eBay, Yahoo and eTrade. DOS attacks occur when a hacker gains control of remotely located computers and uses them to send coordinated message attacks to the target sites, in effect tying up their access points for hours. The FBI reckons total annual losses to hack attacks at $10 billion. They further estimate that most attacks go undetected or unreported.[xxxiv]

The worry is that failure to provide tougher Net security will end its commercial development, especially the movement of financial services to the Net. One thing making it difficult to root out hackers is that many Netizens[xxxv] share the ideological conviction that the Net is designed for community and communal use—it is not really suitable for big business.

Moreover, many would say, "information wants to be free:" in the Net environment, property rights, even privacy concepts, get in the way of the system doing what it does best—letting people work cooperatively. For example, companies track my website use by placing 'cookies' on my machine (unless I explicitly configure my browser to refuse them.) In return for my allowing these trackers, I may get some useful advertising. But the company may also turn the data it collects on its users into a useful mine of information for e-marketers, and not share the profits with those who provided the information. This raises some issues as well.

Whose Information Is It Anyway?

When I give up personal information, I don't surrender every last claim to have a say about what happens to it. A principle of privacy legislation holds that files with personal data will not be linked or combined with others, without the consent of those whose information the files contain, except for statistical purposes where the information cannot be attributed. But this principle is unevenly respected. Some argue that companies should share the gains of their data base transactions with customers who agree to contribute their personal information for that purpose.

In cases of privacy violation and other attempts to acquire and use unauthorized information, governments may themselves be frequent violators. For example, the French government, in particular, cites fears about Project Echelon, an electronic eavesdropping arrangement among the western Allies that dates back at least to the Cold War. Project Echelon has expanded from telephone traffic to include everything that happens on the Net, aided, say the French, by some undocumented design features of US-supplied computer chips. Equally worrisome is the FBI's Carnivore program and new UK security legislation, both of which enlarge the capability of police to read citizens' e-mail. If critics are right about these capabilities, that would make governments the baddest hackers on the block! An example discussed in Chapter 4 is the struggle between the EU and the

US to establish a meeting point on common standards of privacy so that Europeans can feel confident transmitting personal data to companies under US laws.

One way to look at this is to understand that at the margin, the gift culture/business culture clash is a phenomenon of Net life, just like the clashes between nomadic tribes and sedentary tribes, or those between some forms of activity (such as drugs, prostitution and gambling) and straight society, which occur in physical space. Some aspects of this culture clash are damaging, but the two cultures are also symbiotically joined in many ways. The gift culture in particular is crucial to enabling society to make the transition successfully to a Net-based economy. The arms race between hackers and network administrators, while costly and negative, also helps establish the boundaries as to what conduct is and is not acceptable at the margins between the two cultures. Hacker attack and defense is part of a complex system of social re-norming.

Where the Net's New Wealth Comes From

Collective action is the source of considerable new wealth on the Net in forms that our commercial measurement yardsticks cannot evaluate (and that therefore can't be taxed). Just as the medieval city made possible new forms of wealth that meshed uncomfortably with feudal obligations, so it is with cyberspace. These new forms of wealth pose a real challenge to the uniquely consumable products of physical space. In cyberspace, an artists' collective can really be collective and collaborative. Artists can jointly produce products for sale or display. Similarly, consumption can be 'collective' in the sense of shared with whomever wishes to take part. The incentives for this kind of activity revolve around the fun of participation and of realizing a joint project—like decorating a Christmas tree with friends. What isn't clear in this picture is who owns what property rights.

For the people who share this point of view, none of this is about property rights. So how can the free stuff be a form of wealth? Think of it like this:

People are spending (scarce) time, in return for pleasurable interaction. Much of the Internet's resources also empower people and help them do more than they otherwise could. This is wealth in the sense of the gift relationship. Some might even call it 'social capital.' There is a staggering amount of that kind of wealth on the Web, in artists' collectives, self-published fiction, free university course material, as well as the discussions in many and varied newsgroups, much of it amounting to valuable counsel that you might otherwise have to pay for. Perhaps more important, the existence of this free stuff on the Web is what draws people to it—en route they may encounter something that entices them to make a purchase. But the draw to the location comes from the gift side, not the transaction side. The 'malling' of the Web would be far less successful without it. This is 'new wealth.' Our conventional systems have no convenient way of dealing with it any more than feudal systems could deal with money and prices.

Even before the Internet became a social force, there was growing awareness that the individualistic transactions culture, powerful as it is in many ways, offers a second-best solution to many kinds of problems essential for group survival. Such problems involve things that require high-quality inputs at low to zero prices, beyond the competence of single individuals to supply. They can best be supplied by the gift culture. British economist Richard Titmuss made the above-listed points in defense of government-supplied social services 25 years ago in his book *The Gift Culture*. Examples include

- Adequate high-quality blood supply: (Blood can be supplied by the market but that supply will never be as good as that supplied by neighbors for neighbors.)
- Affordable high-quality education. (A commitment to good teaching is not about money.)

- Affordable complex software. (Open source code developed by the user community will outperform and fit more sizes than shrink-wrapped software designed to optimize among different needs.)

- Rewarding emotional connections. (As the song says, "Can't buy me love…")

- Effective political action. (The best Congress money can buy cannot transcend the special interests that pay for special measures.)

The continued predominance of Keynes inspired economic models so generally accepted throughout the 1960s and 70s fueled the assumption that these "gifting" activities need government to coordinate them. We probably wouldn't agree today. While government may still have a role, it will probably be that of putting in place an appropriate legal context. Each of those gift-related services could now be handled through the Internet with only minimal, if any, government involvement. Even on matters as critical as the blood supply, governments have been unable to organize a system themselves and have turned it over to agencies that operate as NGOs with volunteer assistance and some government funding. This is not an argument that the new Net city needs no governance. Rather it is an argument that the old, industrial-style role for government is no longer particularly useful. The next two chapters pursue this theme.

Chapter 6

Are Programs Still Relevant?

"WISDOM is knowing what to do next, SKILL is knowing how to do it, VIRTUE is doing it."

Old Indian Saying

Governments have been struggling with the redesign of public service since at least the late 1980s. New Zealand is generally viewed has having taken the most radical tack, with other parliamentary systems, including Australia, Canada and the UK, studying the example and learning what they could from it. The US has also been inspired by the New Zealand example in its struggles with National Performance Review and Reinventing Government during the Clinton administration. The record has been impressive in terms of efforts at streamlining *process*, but little else. The experience of all jurisdictions has confirmed a number of points:[xxxvi]

- that political systems, which are generally top-down and control-oriented, conflict with theories of bottom-up management and employee empowerment;

- that the main element of accountability in the private sector—economic viability—is not directly applicable to the public sector; and

- that in a period in which policy design and execution involve multiple agencies, jurisdictions and private sector partners, performance accountability is virtually impossible to achieve.

Nevertheless, these redesign exercises are not wasted—on the contrary: new technologies and new approaches can often lead to substantial cost savings. There is also value in documenting difficulties that may be so uncompromising they should be recognized for what they are—insurmountable without a radical change in government itself. Chief among these is finding some rationale, apart from politics, to justify the choice of government activity.

Government reform efforts emerged as a response to plummeting citizen confidence and growing tax revolts in the 1970s and 80s. To some extent, they were also prompted by the critiques of economists and 'public choice' political scientists. A central criticism of a market-based economy is that entrepreneurial business people act in their own interests, and are therefore greedy, whereas government officials are motivated by the unselfish desire to serve the public. Therefore, government policy is unselfish and in the public interest.

Public choice theory holds that government bureaucrats can also be selfish and greedy and act in their own interests—they do not make policy in a pure cloud that sits above the economy. Its adherents say that in fact, it is 'public policy entrepreneurs,' capturing the rule-making monopoly of government to maximize benefits for themselves or their organizations, who drive modern government. Public choice theory explains one of the biggest mysteries that theories based on 'the public good' never could: why there were no brakes on public sector expansion within the political system. (Capital markets, alarmed by the accumulated debts and deficits run up by democratic governments, provided the brakes when they drew the line on new spending.)

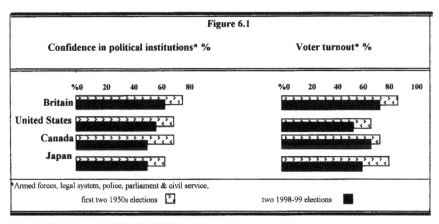

Figure 6.1

Confidence in political institutions* %

Voter turnout* %

*Armed forces, legal system, police, parliament & civil service,

first two 1950s elections

two 1998-99 elections

Source: *The Economist July 17, 1999*

Under purely public interest theories of government, government is held to be a defender of freedom and disinterested stabilizer acting always for the public good. If this theory were true, governments should have shown more responsibility and accountability in halting their own expansion well before it imperiled national and international economic systems. The failure of government accountability in practice led to the attempts at re-establishing reform and accountability through government re-invention. There has been some progress in tightening up a situation that had grown far too loose. But there has been no real progress in solving the fundamental issues.

This outcome is not astonishing if one remembers that governments are political systems, designed to solve political problems through a careful balancing of political pressures. The accountability problems have arisen from a fundamental confusion about the roles of government and markets. Given the history of the mid-20th century, it is not surprising that this confusion arose, for it seemed that public policy (in the form of government programs) could re-establish markets and help them become more stable. Policies conceived in the spirit of the New Deal and Keynesian economics justified the expansion of government through programs as a response to 'market failures.' At the same time, the program interventions achieved an important political goal as well—papering over cracks between capital and labor that seemed endemic to industrial capitalism.

The most important interventions were to provide income support for the destitute (welfare), income maintenance for the temporarily jobless (unemployment insurance), shelter for the homeless (public housing) and, gradually, access to the advantages of privilege, such as medical coverage and post-secondary education. Until World War II, private charity, self-insurance and (for education) diligent private saving were the main suppliers. Government's responsibility was limited to ensuring price stability, national defense and the proper operation of the justice system, including the maintenance of competition and fair trading. The Depression was so devastating that the private systems were simply overwhelmed. Not only the vulnerable wage-dependent working class and small farmers, but also propertied middle-class savers and professionals were wiped out and threatened with permanent destitution. The New Deal and its copycat programs elsewhere represented democracy's best response to the totalitarian solutions of Germany, Italy and the Soviet Union.

At start-up, those programs could be justified for the Depression generation, who fought and won the most awful war in history. For one thing, many of them, like their parents, had lacked an opportunity to save and put together a viable retirement plan because of the world calamities. That was not the case for most of the following generation, the baby boomers, for whom the same benefits were promised. Inevitably, the promise of permanent government benefits eroded to some extent their incentive to save. Encouraged as teen-agers, the baby boomers have excelled as consumers of increasingly expensive and elaborate products that have proliferated in variety and number. This proliferation of products actually conferred a major public good on the consuming public—contrary to many predictions in the 70s. Private enterprise, instead of consolidating into longer, more efficient product lines, has diversified into broader product categories with much greater freedom of choice. To get an idea of how much variety has exploded onto consumer markets, look at the table below.

The same diversity has spilled over into goods and services supplied through governments as well. In medical care in particular, the explosion of medical science and increasing knowledge about disease and its treatment has led to a growing variety of possible solutions. The habits of a lifetime of rampant consumption, gratified by an ever-widening variety of things to buy, have made most of us unwilling to constrain the choices available to us. If we see a product that meets our specific needs, we expect to be able to obtain it. If we can't afford it right now, we expect the supplier to make it affordable eventually.

Today's citizens are not about to accept restrictions on medical choice based on the decisions made upstream by a government-directed supplier. On the contrary, consumers will hit the Net to see what else is out there, and in the absence of reasons they accept, will want to try what looks best to them. Given the expansion of medical therapies and the ability of people to find them, it is not surprising that today's doctors are actually coming to count on patients bringing novel remedies to their attention. In many cases, however, when the doctor turns to the insurer—either the American HMO or in Canada the provincial government health plan—she's told that the plan doesn't cover the remedy.

Public institutions are not organized to cater to 'mass customization.' Worse, when they try it, the exceptions often create additional political problems. Narrow or specific program targeting is often perceived as confusion or unfairness in policy (why should hunting and fishing rules be different for native peoples than for non-native Canadians? Why should some regions of the country sentence some crimes more harshly than others?) Governments have trouble coming up with solutions that match individual cases, even though technology offers more choices for consumers, especially in such big-ticket items as medicine and education.

Government programs are limited in the degree to which they can depart from the one-size-fits-all basis, if only because all taxpayers feel they are equal under the law. To be sure, we all pay different amounts of tax, but giving the rich more benefits because they pay more tax is seen as a violation—indeed, most people believe the reverse should be true.

Table 6.2 Proliferation of Consumer Goods over the Past Quarter Century		
Item	**Early 70s**	**Late 90s**
Vehicle models	140	260
Movie releases	267	458
Magazine titles	339	790
New book titles	40,530	77,446
TV screen sizes	5	15
McDonald's menu items	13	43
KFC menu items	7	14
Frito-Lay chip varieties	10	78
Breakfast cereals	160	340
Pop-Tarts	3	29
Milk types	4	19
Bottled water brands	19	50
National soft drink brands	20	87
Colgate toothpastes	2	17
Dental flosses	12	64

Source: Excerpted from *The Right Stuff*, Federal Reserve Bank of Dallas, 1999, in *Fraser Forum*, Fraser Institute, July 1999

Now globalization and the Internet have emerged to lay some stark choices on the table. The power of governments to oblige people to pay for programs they don't wish to support is less than it was and diminishing rapidly. People will increasingly avail themselves of the right—whether governments permit it or not — to organize their affairs so that the tax they pay is roughly equal to the value they get back. As more and more work is done over the Internet and across borders, governments will find themselves subject to what amounts to private-sector-style accountability and the reality of taxpayer desertion.

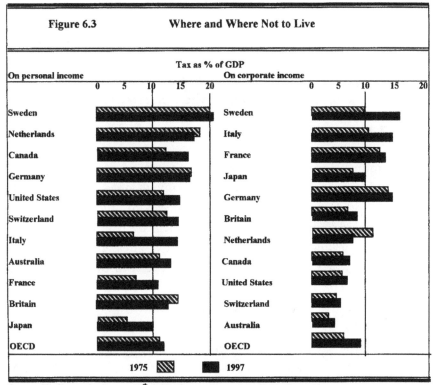

Figure 6.3   **Where and Where Not to Live**

Tax as % of GDP

Source: *The Economist*, January 29th, 2000, "Survey: Tax and the Net", after p. 64

Many governments have already begun to adjust to this reality occurring in the corporate sector. As globalization has expanded, corporate nominal tax rates have been dropping and governments have become increasingly less dependent on corporate tax revenue. Governments have been lowering their corporate tax rates so as to attract, through competition, greater levels of corporate investment. Probably Ireland is the clear winner in this battle and high-tax jurisdictions like Germany the clear losers. As mentioned earlier, the EU and the OECD alike are trying to reduce 'harmful' tax competition among governments—effectively trying to block corporate taxpayers from equating tax 'prices' and benefits at the margin. At the same time, however, those governments have also been raising taxes on sources they consider captive—namely, individuals like us. This harmonization strategy of high-tax countries will probably fail through unenforceability, however, even if it succeeds on paper. The Internet enables those who work with ideas (just about everyone these days) to set up their affairs to 'work' (or record their sales) where they like.

Social Issues, Social Programs

Short of money and forced to compete on ideas, governments have little choice but to reconfigure (if not exit) many income-maintenance and other social programs. One approach might seek to privatize the income-maintenance programs or else to finance them by making the programs themselves appealing to capital markets. We've already seen that capital markets are not friendly to governments that seek to use their own borrowing capacity to finance deficits. It may, however, be possible to design social programs that have their own market appeal. In other words, if programs can't be maintained from current expenditures, then the programs—not the government—might be financed. This would be a big change, and might lead to social programs being sliced and diced to appeal to *investors'* appetites.

The common aim of innovative approaches would be to let the private sector offer as wide a variety of maintenance programs as the market could bear, with governments filling in along the margins and at the high-risk ends where they could still add financial value. Can this be done, and what would be the financial burden?

Surprisingly, on a net basis, most governments spend about the same as a proportion of GDP. What varies is how much they tax back in order to pay for program delivery. Here's the pattern, as shown by a recent OECD study.

Table 6.4	Gross and Net Social Expenditure (% GDP) Selected OECD Countries	
	Gross Social Expenditure	Net Social Expenditure
Canada	20.8	21.2
Germany	30.4	27.7
Sweden	36.4	27.0
UK	25.9	26.0
US	17.1	24.5

Sources: Willem Adema, Labor Market and Social Policy–Occasional papers Occasional PapersNo. 39 Net Social Expenditure, OECD, August 1999 DEELS/ELSA/WD(99)3, Table 7, Net Social Expenditure Indicators, 1993-95, as a percentage of GDP at factor cost, p.31

It's particularly noteworthy that the US, generally regarded as a low-baller on social programs, outspends Canada on an after-tax basis. Sweden (supposedly generous) and the UK (supposedly stingy) are within one percentage point of each other on an after-tax basis. Much of the supposed generosity of the big social spenders camouflages the impact of the tax system: in order to pay for the state-controlled delivery of publicly supplied programs, the tax system claws back much of the outlay. The same study also shows the claw-back rates on selected programs.

These tables show the high cost of targeting in most government systems. Counter-intuitively, the two tables together show that the low-tax countries are just as generous as the high-tax countries, whereas one might have expected that the highest-tax countries would redistribute the most income. The difference is that the high-tax countries pay a great deal more to target programs than low-tax countries, which provide more universal access to benefits without the same tax-related claw-backs. Targeting enables net

Table 6.5	Indirect Tax and Claw-back Rates (%GDP) Selected OECD Countries			
	Indirect taxes	UI or EI	Sickness benefits	Private pension benefits
Canada	16.8	21.9	21.9	28.3
Germany	19.1	0	32.7	10.8
Sweden	23.0	30.8	31.4	28.5
UK	19.9	0.6	21.1	12.2
US	7.5	5.9	22.3	7.6

Source: loc cit

benefits to the targeted groups to be more generous, but the programs cost more to operate. Moreover, the income thresholds block the mobility of the target group and create disincentives to move off the programs.[xxxvii]

Why do governments stick to these programs, anyway? Taxpayers may prefer them as a check on government waste. High marginal rates make taxpayers very aware of the real value of last tax dollars they pay: the more money a taxpayer has to pay, the more pressure she puts on governments to make sure there's value for money in the system. If an individual pays twice as much tax in Canada as in the US, she wants assurance that (1) the money is going where it will do the most good and that (2) public policy goals are being met. Thus, program targeting becomes a strategy for maintaining public acceptance of high tax rates rather than achieving program goals such as eliminating or minimizing poverty. But there is a deeper issue at work: whether the poverty is structural or cyclical. If it's structural, programs should aim at effective maintenance until the structural problems can be successfully addressed. Therefore targeting may seem like the best option—even if it entrenches the structural problem. If poverty is cyclical, an acceleration of economic growth will take care of getting the poor back into the work force. Low-tax countries believe they can let expansion of their macro-economies do the redistribution by reducing dependence on the programs: they can thus afford to spend much less on program design and administration.

If this is the situation now, what will be the effect of making taxes even more voluntary? The likelihood is high that more money would flow to the tax base of the low-tax regimes—not because taxpayers are selfish but because entrepreneurial spirits see the opportunity costs intrinsic to high-cost targeted systems. But governments that want to target can ask another question: how much of the social program portfolio can be self-financed in the market and how much needs to depend on net tax receipts? Money flowing out of the country as lost tax revenue may flow back in as investment in self-financing programs. Either way, by this reasoning, one impact of a more mobile tax base would be to reduce government's role in social programs—either by cutting administration and reducing targeting or by letting the private market fund more of the targeted programs. (This is discussed in more detail in Chapter 8.) Gradually, governments will be 'dis-intermediated'—no longer the link between taxpayers and the disadvantaged. Either the program administrators will be cut back as program targeting fades away or investors, rather than taxpayers, will fund large portions of programs directly. Happily, there may be better alternatives.

One clear alternative to this process would be for governments and civil society to work together on building positive social processes that minimize the number of people who actually find themselves vulnerable to conditions of exclusion and deprivation. If this is to occur, ordinary people must be ready to take an interest in the disadvantaged and excluded, and not leave matters entirely up to government. Happily for the tax system, this interest need not be tax-funded—indeed, it would probably work best if government played only a supervisory, monitoring role and let civil society design as well as implement the programs.

Civil Society Seeks Involvement

There's another side to social programs besides the pressure on government resources. Not only is government facing pressures from taxpayers to reduce their funding involvement with social programs, there's also increasing pressures from the new civil society that wants to get involved—often with innovative fund raising activities and other interventions that make extensive use of the Internet.

For example, we're beginning to see electronic auction structures along the lines of eBay emerging for donors, complete with the annual reports and other proofs of accomplishment displayed by civil organizations. Click on *www.netaid.org* and you'll see an example in embryo. For an up-to-date look at other volunteer and public service opportunity, check out *www.idealist.com*. As well, companies are using donations as inducements to reply to Web-based surveys, and other sites are using innovative methods for promoting contributions to meet social goals. One example is the UN food aid site *www.hungersite.com*. For an overview of the Canadian situation, visit *www.volunteer.ca*

These sites and activities represent another deep public policy trend—the need to consult, work with and ultimately rely on stakeholder groups to design and assist with the implementation of public policy.

This has emerged not altogether out of government altruism, but rather from the fact that the new civil society is more effective than are most government agencies. Government has no special expertise in regard to real-life social problems. Most governments don't put blankets on homeless people, and the average health minister is pretty useless in a hospital ER. In many of these instances, government acts as the intermediary between the recipients of tax aid and the contributor or donor.

The advent of nearly universal access to PCs and the Net also allows these stakeholder groups and their friends to be more effective politically than are most government agencies. An umbrella civic action group like the Council of Canadians draws on a wide network of volunteer action groups, from Greenpeace and farm organizations to labor unions and their research centers. While bureaucrats have to vet every statement for political acceptability, civic action organizations simply videotape their conferences and statements and put that on the Web without much regard to exacting details. While their arguments often suffer as a result, this is more than offset by their visibility.

In any case, many citizens now feel so disconnected from policy that arguments matter less than appearance. The action groups' very visibility gives them a trump card over the private, and often more knowledgeable, special-interest lobbyists. In a micro-short length of time the new civic action groups can take over the mind-space most busy citizens have to allocate to these things. Inevitably governments must turn to these organizations as partners in program development and implementation. Action groups now often have more direct access to senior power than do the program managers in the ministries.

It's therefore only a matter of time before governments have to face the question, "Why not withdraw altogether from program implementation and return it to civic action groups?" Expanding the income tax charity deduction would allow the groups to compete for public support and that, in turn, would increase the accountability of the groups. It would also allow governments to focus on *outcomes* (as distinct from bureaucrats' *outputs*) that could be affected by program design.

In other words, if it's a priority to eliminate homelessness, why not rely on civil society? Civic groups can handle the design, construction and management of such new housing as may be required. Volunteer groups can coordinate the delivery of the various types of social assistance individuals may need. They can also develop the day care and other facilities some portion of the homeless population requires to get back to leading healthy and productive lives. Government may have a role as a convener—especially if different levels of government are required and legislation is needed—but citizens can take charge of these things and make them happen far more effectively than government departments. Conversely, governments can legitimately worry about whether the civic groups are actually achieving the desired outcomes.

To some extent this is happening already. NGOs are involved in a wide range of issues. They deal with immigration policy; social programs such as aid to the homeless, the disabled, runaway children, and street people; food banks; more traditional endeavors such as Little League, kids' hockey, summer camps and local hospitals; as well as more dramatic interventions around the world in support of UN programs. There are clear social benefits from having a strong volunteer network as the basis of society. It bridges the gap between classes and humanizes the advantaged and disadvantaged alike. Our grandparents understood this. To the Victorians, volunteer work was so gratifying that they often paid for the privilege. It's probably true that, as with the blood supply, a healthy, high quality civic culture has to come from volunteers. You can't buy it with expensive social programs. It has to be supplied by the gift culture.

The importance of the Net is that it is explicitly designed to facilitate the coming together of groups to promote common solutions. Stepping out of the loop of program design and delivery, but insisting upon verifiable performance standards, is a useful role for governments and would help us find effective solutions to social problems. Clearly, however, there will be a political challenge in getting there.

These reflections also raise a broader point that underlines the importance of this change. Taking governments out of the loop between taxpayers who *have* to pay for programs and the supposed beneficiaries of government programs, and replacing the tax dollars with volunteers who *want* to be there, is a big change. It's not just an issue of making social programs more effective. It's also part of a revolutionary turnaround in the way societies conduct themselves.

The baby-boom generation was raised to think of government as the supplier of everything essential in life—from education to food stamps. The safety-net concept kept most of us both 'secure' and 'insecure' in an abstract sense, like having an absent parent, such as Orphan Annie's Daddy Warbucks. In the same sense it lifted from our shoulders any real involvement with the fate of our neighbors. If people got into trouble, they could rely on the safety net. Right now, we have no real civic obligation other than to pay taxes. We coast on the efforts of those who, regardless of the safety net, take responsibility for the health of their communities. Fortunately, as the boomers age, there's every sign this pool of volunteers will increase.

Shifting the Burden of Risk

In making its promises to more than the wartime generation, the welfare state made an additional fundamental change in the way society was run.

It significantly distorted the treatment of risk in society. This is another area where globalization and the Net will have a major impact through dis-intermediating the role of the state.

One of the most important consequences of communities moving to the Internet, one that underpins many of the institutional changes, is the impact on how risk is distributed in society. Historically, the growth of the state has been accompanied by its increasing assumption of risk. Until the 20th century, most of the risks of life that ordinary people faced were relatively uncontrollable. Medicine was not very useful against disease or injury; economies were as much controlled by custom as by markets. Not much could be done about these.

The state was a relatively small actor whose chief threats were jail and war. Most of the controllable risks facing ordinary people came down to bad marriage, personal debt, personal injury (at work or in society from riding accidents and dueling), and the risk of fire destroying personal property. For women, death in childbirth needs to be added, as well as the risk of poverty in old age—the stuff of many 19th century novels. These risks were all assumed by individuals; social mores developed to enable people to live prudently and minimize controllable risks, since there was no other entity to assume them.

The struggle for nationhood in Germany, the strength of the trade union movement, the big wars of this century, the improvements in medical care, and above all, the growing role of the state in economic management changed all this. The welfare state—especially the post World War II variety—assumed most of the risk run by normal adults in industrial society. Medicare, unemployment insurance, family allowances, state-sponsored relief services—these meant that risks run by North Americans as recently as the 1930s were now assumed by the state. Unlike the Depression generation, the boomers and their children have never had to worry much about the financial consequences of personal risk. The large government debts that resulted from the state's assumption of risk became the assets of private insurance company portfolios and pension plans—they have historically been the buyers of short- and long-term government debt.

Now, however, globalization, the weakening financial capacity of the state, and the financial services revolution of the 1980s have all intersected in a way that returns the burden of risk to individuals. The issue is more fundamental than a simple decline in social program spending. To see what's happened, let's look at how risk is assumed.

When the welfare state was established, currency rates were fixed, international capital flows were controlled, and international trade was relatively minor in its impact on domestic economies. Social programs were part of a series of so-called 'stabilizers' that would be triggered by an economic downturn. In theory, the additional spending by governments would prevent a recession from becoming a 1930s-style economic collapse. The return of prosperity would pay down the public debt that had been incurred during lean times.

The state thus assumed the bulk of economic risk arising from cyclical fluctuations in economic growth. As well, the programs assured local credit granters (the banker, the baker) that even if a breadwinner lost his job, the family was able to settle its basic expenses until things picked up again. Added to this were state-supported medical programs—the risk of disease and injury was now assumed in financial terms by the state. Medical care was available at no financial burden.

Supplementing the government assumption of risk was the insurance industry: it added supplementary medical benefits to its traditional offerings of life, auto, property and casualty insurance. Under these plans, insurance companies assumed any additional risk. Insurance companies are, by their very nature, risk owners. They seek out risks to buy. For an insurance company, any risk that can be measured and assumed by someone can be insured.

This was a natural expansion for the insurance industry. From their beginnings insuring ships at sea, insurance companies were naturally led into the property and casualty business. Compared to the risks of those businesses, life insurance was straightforward, as were annuities. All these businesses are much like the banking business, balancing outgoing payments against incoming payments, although the risk profiles are more complicated than with simple deposit-taking and short-term lending. Still, in maritime insurance, successful voyages have to pay for the unsuccessful ones. In property and casualty insurance, the lucky ones have to pay for the unlucky ones; in life insurance, the premiums have to cover the promise to the beneficiaries. In each of these cases, the insurance company occupies the middle—it takes the risk, redistributing it with other insurance companies if the risks look too great.

Before the welfare state, since any serious injury carried with it the risk of death, life insurance was almost the only coverage a responsible person needed. Besides insurance companies that issued life policies to the middle class, mutual societies emerged to offer more limited, cheaper coverage to working-class men. With the advent of the welfare state, the private insurance industry saw much of the risk it used to cover—and a lot of the risk it had felt was too hard to cover—pass into the tax-supported sector. As a consequence, the insurance industry was left with the relatively upside of the market—people who could afford additional coverage—as well as lots of risk-free capital in the form of government debt, for them to recycle in the form of new insurance products. The 1980s revolution in banking and financial services, combined with the weakening of the state, has returned the burden of risk assumption to the individual.

To see how this occurred, we need to take a closer look at what we call the disintermediation of banking—taking the bank out of its role as the link between lenders and borrowers. In the early years of the century, this was its primary function: you put your money in the bank, and the bank paid you interest on the deposit. The bank then lent your money to a borrower, for a higher rate of interest. As long as the borrower paid down his debt on time and the depositor kept his money in the bank, everything worked fine.

After the massive number of American bank closings in the Great Depression, the government ordered that a deposit insurance pool be set up by the banking system. Although no national banks in Canada collapsed during the Depression, the Canadian government echoed the US with a similar deposit insurance measure. Thus, if a borrower declares personal bankruptcy, deposits are guaranteed (up to $100,000 in the US, $60,000 in Canada), and the risk of the loan is borne by the banks.

While deposit insurance still exists, banks' main function is no longer one of intermediary. They still lend money, but now they collect their loans together, and with the help of computers, slice and dice them to create synthetic financial products that can be sold in capital markets. In other words, they 'securitize' their loans. The buyers of those securities undertake the risk of default. The bank thus has no more risk. It has dis-intermediated itself—taken itself out of the middle of the transaction and passed the risk on to the security buyer.

The bottom line is this: with the bank in the middle, all or almost all risk would be borne by the bank. Without the bank in the middle, the risk is sustained by the others in the transaction chain—the buyer of the certificate and the mortgage holder making the payments. Since the revolution in banking and finance of the 1980s, banks have been aggressively seeking this kind of risk management activity. Indeed, banks and investment dealers now undertake to engineer financial products to meet almost any risk /reward profile desired. But in so doing, they do not take the risk themselves. They are risk *managers*, not owners.

The welfare state effectively promised to eliminate the insurable risks of life's events. Cradle-to-grave security supplied by the state would have exceeded its fiscal capacity immediately, had it been supplied on an actuarially sound basis. Instead, social programs were supplied on a pay-as-you-go basis, on the assumption of a perpetually expanding work force. Governments kept issuing bonds to finance ever-increasing deficits.

This environment provided opportunities for insurance companies. It enabled them to invest over the long term in relatively high-return government securities at low risk. This encouraged industry to offer coverage at lower-than-realistic rates, confident they could make up the difference through investments. And they could do it with impunity, since the welfare state also protected the insurance industry from competition by passing legislation that kept out other segments of the financial services industry.

By the mid-1990s, little of this environment remained. Governments were reducing their borrowing, other financial institutions were allowed to sell insurance, and financial services had evolved in a way that vastly increased business without assuming new risk. That's where we are today. As banks and other competitors move into the insurance segment, they will probably do so with financial products in which they have no intermediary role. An investment fund, for example, provides nest-egg accumulation like an insurance policy. But the risks are borne by the owner. Such products can provide the same or better return with zero risk to the provider. This puts competitive pressure on traditional insurance products. To withstand these pressures, the insurance industry must itself reorganize, which it is doing by de-mutualizing—that is, changing its organizational form so that it can raise capital in the stock market and, in quite a few cases, become acquired by a larger, mega-financial company.

The transformation of the insurance industry provides an interesting complement to the changing approach to governance and to the assumption of risk in society. The social contribution of insurance is that it pools individual risks, so that the relatively dangerous activities of society can be offset against the more humdrum tasks. When society wishes to advance, the risks can be priced and the charge on the nation's resources computed. From the age of sail to that of jumbo jets, the risks of human progress were covered by the insurance industry through risk pooling. Now, if the insurance industry effectively disappears because of dis-inter-mediation, what happens?

Perhaps it could be argued that one result would be less risky financial markets. When risk pools no longer constitute the normal way for society to manage risk, financial markets may become safer, because instead of a few big insurers that could go down, there are thousands of self-insurers whose individual losses will not likely affect the health of the system as a whole. Yet that's not much help to ordinary people.

At the same time, without a formal insurance sector, society would no longer be able to pool risk to the same degree. Those with normal risks and average means would be unable to insure to the same extent as before. Similarly, great endeavors that might have been achieved would have to be called off, unless the parties could self-insure. Above all, it means that a major vehicle by which society has always managed the risks of life must find a new way to prosper, or disappear. The most important, bottom-line result: risk passes back to ordinary consumers.

Trade Union Role

One surprising possibility is that the trade union movement could move in to supply what the conventional insurance industry does not. The unions blazing this trail are generally in the entertainment industry, whose business model, even before the information age, most closely resembles info-age models. The Writers' Guild of America (WGA) and the Association of Canadian Television and Radio Actors (ACTRA) both began as traditional unions, and still perform many traditional union functions. But in the 1990s, when commercial insurers couldn't meet the requirements for insurance and Blue Cross proved to be too expensive, these organizations morphed into complex financial institutions, adminis-tering plans for non-member groups to earn fees that subsidize member benefits. In addition, ACTRA is a registered insurance company, investing its premium assets in order to pay member claims. These trail-blazing organizations have assumed the management of their risk, and are doing what most successful information-age companies are doing: they are partnering to become more competitive and to drive down costs, and they are looking for every opportunity to grow.

And Now...?

How well are markets adjusting to the general question of the moving burden of risk? Consider, for example, the way people save for their old age. In the US and Canada, conventional savings rates are lower than they used to be, but investment in equities, especially through mutual funds, is higher. If the capital in mutual funds were translated back into bank deposits in savings accounts, the volume of deposits would increase by 50 per cent. Perhaps people invest in mutual funds because they think the government-promised, compulsorily financed pensions will either not be there or be too small to provide a comfortable retirement. Indeed, a growing trend is to scrap company pensions with defined benefits altogether as too burdensome on the company, and let people manage their own pensions in the form of defined contributions to professionally managed pension funds.

But there's a difference: equities go down as well as up. Unlike government obligations and life insurance, the risks are borne by the owner. Paradoxically, the retirement savings of a generation whose old age has been largely insured by governments are tied up in a stock market that could go down as fast as it goes up. The question is how to evaluate this behavior. Do individuals take on new risks because they lack confidence in the state's promises? Or are we looking at additional risk assumption because, bottom line, the investors believe some kind of a nest egg will always be there, in the form of state-sponsored social security? The same conundrum also applies to the assets underlying insurance policies. For as government debt diminishes, the closest things to low-risk bonds are so-called 'blue chip' stocks. As the market moves towards equities, it increasingly offloads risk onto consumers.

The bottom line here is this: globalization and changes in financial markets are re-allocating risk away from the state precisely when the Internet and the dispersal of enterprise are weakening the state's capacity to deliver on its promises. Gradually, consciously or unconsciously, ordinary people are assuming greater responsibility for their own lives. What's more, the same trends that are propelling these changes are making it easier for people to organize in communities of interest in order to affect their own environments. They're doing this through a combination of social, political and economic actions. These add up to powerful forces for keeping government in the rule-making business, but out of programs.

What about the health of our communities? Increasingly, as people take on more risk, they will also take on more responsibility for managing those risks. Social mores will become more risk averse. Marriages will last longer. Children will be better cared for and develop responsibility earlier. Opportunities for active community involvement will increase along with social pressure to participate. The gift culture will take back community life in the Internet Age.

Chapter 7

The Death of Policy

"So far, in rich countries, policymakers have been notably reluctant to reconsider from first principles what role the state should play in pensions, health care and the rest. Yet the time is ripe for a fundamental rethink."
—Mathew Bishop, Social Insurance Survey, *The Economist,*
Oct. 24, 1998

Policy – as the word suggests—is the heart of politics. Since the time of the city-state or *polis*, the victors in politics have made policies that reflected their priorities. Policy is therefore about rules and decisions— choices made by political winners and choices they enforce on the rest of us. Throughout the political community the winners control: be it city, state or nation. Yet despite the partisan nature of politics and a mountain of historical evidence that policies basically favor winners (starting with Plato's famous four-stage political cycle set out in *The Republic*) economic policy debates are usually presented as the exception. Even the phrase 'public policy' has been shorn of its overt political connotations, in that policy is supposed to be scientific and divorced from grubby old politics, the preoccupation of spin-doctors, lobbyists and party hacks.

Apparently divorced from the baser political concerns, economic debates about public policy are generally couched in references to the general welfare or the public good, using rhetoric strangely denatured and stripped of partisan color. Everyone has heard these interminable debates: "tax cuts are good for everyone," "a rising tide lifts all boats," or "tax cuts are bad," "governments are best placed to make infrastructure investments the country needs," and so on. The belief, reinforced by economists (who as a professional group now dominate these discussions), is that governments have a special ability to see and act on the broader picture, and above all can conduct their operations so as to stabilize and improve the operation and efficiency of private markets.

Even Adam Smith, the first of the free market advocates, believed that certain expenditures were appropriate to the state. These included keeping weights and measures accurate and ensuring the defense of the realm—expenses that were for the general benefit. But it wasn't until the first half of the 20th century that economists began to look seriously at public policy and devise concepts and tools whereby policy-makers could supposedly make better, more informed and less ideologically driven choices about the general welfare. Not surprisingly, that branch of economics is known as 'public economics' or 'welfare economics'—policy with the politics left out. The ascendancy of public economics, and in particular the credibility of its claims to scientific objectivity, accompanied the rise of the welfare state. Ironically, even critiques by other economic schools such as public choice serve to strengthen the belief in some quarters that there is an optimal economic policy that can be determined by scientific means alone.

This edifice of economic reasoning was based on assumptions rooted in the information flows of industrial society and reflected in the nation-state. These assumptions no longer apply in a global economy based on ideas and ubiquitous information. As a result, many of the core intellectual concepts underlying post-war economic policy can no longer be applied without significant adaptation and adjustment—essentially, rein-vention. In effect, policy—at least as we used to understand it—is dead.

Natural Monopoly

The first of the old ideas about government regulation to fall was that of 'natural monopoly.' This was the term economists applied to industries that required a large amount of capital investment to reach efficient scale: that is, to become large enough to supply a product efficiently. According to this view, some industries were of such a scale that there could only be one efficient supplier in a particular market. Adding other suppliers would simply waste money without adding to efficiency. Indeed, competition might reduce efficiency. One example of this was the transcontinental rail-way. One railway could achieve full economies of scale over a whole national network. The savings could be passed on to consumers by ensur-ing that rates were properly regulated. Two railroads would cost passengers or shippers twice as much as one, because duplication and competition would forestall the economies possible with a regulated monopoly.

Over time, this argument migrated from railroads to telecommunications, to power utilities, to national airlines, indeed, state enterprises of a wide variety. All were (or still are) overseen by regulatory commissions instead of setting prices in the marketplace through competition-based efficiency. For about 100 years, sophisticated people believed this argument. Its validity has died with open markets, privatization and globalization. Investment liberalization has led to startling improvements in services and technologies that were once deemed natural monopolies. In the middle-income countries, deregulation of telecommunications (along with priva-tization of former state monopolies) has led to a vastly better telecommunications infrastructure, a rapid increase of available services and a steep decline in overall telecommunications costs. This in turn has stimulated foreign investment and the creation of economically viable world-class production facilities—all within a few short years. Clearly a lot more remains to be done, but countries like Hungary, Chile, Mexico and Argentina, to name but a few, are making rapid progress because they abandoned the old natural monopoly models.

One key to the change is the effect of non-discriminatory market access for investors. With international competition to provide what national competition could not, and with scale economies possible at unprecedented levels across international markets, there was no market too small to attract capital on some basis. From the 1980s to the present day, debt-strapped states have been selling off government-run and government-controlled entities and using the money to strengthen the national balance sheet. Competition has allowed these newly privatized businesses to grow, with demand rising and prices falling.

The countries that have benefited most are the two that moved first to scrap the natural monopoly models—the US and the UK. They now have the most advanced telecommunications infrastructures in the world and are reaping huge gains by applying the new possibilities this opens in every other area. The 2000 takeover of Time Warner by an Internet provider, AOL, and the fusion of the biggest cell-phone companies in Europe under British Vodafone leadership are examples of new-economy companies accelerating change through competitive markets. Competition, not regulated monopoly, leads to the greatest variety of services at the least price for the best value. Even more important for our understanding of this digitized information age is to examine the impact of easy access to Infocosm services on other basic concepts of welfare economics.

Public Goods

As the expansion of information technology into the lives of ordinary people continues, so the concept of government-supplied public goods becomes less readily applicable. These are supposed to be goods that are jointly consumed—that is, if such a good exists, then everyone enjoys it. Its consumption, in the jargon, is non-excludable. The classic example is national defense. Whether an individual or a government supplies it, everyone in the country is automatically covered. National defense defends the country and everyone in it simultaneously. You can't buy just a kilo or two of defense—the whole budget needs to be covered and then the whole country is protected. Now the logic here is more important than the specific case. Because the product is jointly consumed, the market can't supply it. There is no buyer; no one can own it. Therefore, no individual will pay for it, because he would pay while everyone else gets a free ride. According to classical welfare economics, this class of goods will make everyone better off, and yet it cannot be market-supplied. Government must supply it.

Perhaps the best way to illustrate these points is with the most basic example, that of the lighthouse. Imagine a rocky cove close to a major port where ships fairly regularly run aground. The cost of erecting a lighthouse is more than the individual shippers want to pay, partly because they know if someone builds it, all will benefit. The possibility of getting a free ride kills the incentive to construct the lighthouse. So government steps in and levies a lighthouse tax that compels the shippers to contribute to the construction of the lighthouse in proportion to their shipping volume.

Now let's see the effect of new technology. Today the lighthouse can be replaced by a satellite-based positioning system that will warn boats if they are going to pass too close to the rocks. Say that to make the satellite work, each ship needs a transponder—an electronic black box—that translates the satellite signal into a position and visual track on-screen for the helmsman. As you have to buy the transponder to get the signal, there are no free rides. A powerful inducement to buy one would be a decrease in shipping insurance rates for boats that have a transponder installed. Competitive pressures to lower costs create the market for transponders that finances the launch and maintenance of the satellite system. What used to be a market failure becomes a successful private market, in the presence of technology that addresses the problem. The new technology makes most public goods addressable and thereby excludable. Therefore, the penetration of the new technology makes possible the market supply of a class of policies that hitherto could only be efficiently supplied by government.

Logic would suggest that government should exit the direct supply of most public services and concentrate on the development of such pure public goods as may remain—keeping markets efficient, keeping the legal system functioning appropriately, etc. In many countries, this transition from government service supply to private service supply is already underway. In the US, private companies handle welfare program delivery and are paid for their ability to clear up welfare caseloads and help recipients get back into the job market. In Canada, it is clear from recent provincial announcements that the way is opening for greater private-sector participation in post-secondary education and health care. In Alberta and Ontario in particular, provincial governments are clearing the way for charter schools. In Alberta the way is being opened for the private supply of health care as a supplement to the supply available within the existing system.

Another development is the emergence of distance education that is ready for prime time. This will have a dramatic impact on government policy. Free trade in educational services is still restricted under WTO agreements—foreign suppliers are not entitled yet to non-discriminatory national treatment. But as the rules on services liberalize, this will change. The impact will inevitably be to shift government subsidies from schools to students, letting them choose the accredited supplier irrespective of national origin. The liberalization of education will be of tremendous value to countries around the world that do not have access to the capital needed to bring their educational systems up to world standards. It will vastly increase the educational opportunities for those who need it most.

Moving away from the traditional public goods model to an efficient public goods *supply* model will change policy itself. Here's how. At the heart of the concept of public goods is the 'non-excludability' concept: in order for society to benefit, society must pay. In fact, however, that only applies when there are no other benefits attached to the service. One difference between the satellite-transponder and the lighthouse example is that the technology created a means to provide a general warning on an exclusive basis. The increase in general safety nevertheless remained a non-excludable public good. In the example of education services, a steep increase in choice and availability from offshore distance learning enhances the public goods objectives that flow from an educated population. But the variety and quality of the new services will be such that the choice of acceptability has to be left to the students. Finding ways to improve competitive market operation will do more to keep costs low and increase supply than any policy could achieve. The need to rethink traditional public goods approaches to policy-making is urgent and growing more so with every passing day.

Regulation and Risk Assessment

In today's economy, innovation is the key to competitive advantage. In most advanced countries, industry conducts the lion's share of scientific research, a change in the last 10 years as government budgets have come under increasing scrutiny. Consequently, science has changed. It's still about inspired, seriously involved people with amazing insights into their fields. But now the rate of scientific knowledge in medicine, biotechnology, information technology and many other fields is doubling every two years or less. And therein lies yet another challenge to traditional public goods policy models.

Confidence in innovation and improving public health are the public goods that governments are trying to achieve by acting as gatekeepers on new products. But the system is collapsing around us. There is no way for in-house government expertise in every country to evaluate the stream of new applications for all these advances. As well, the outside evaluators who are on the cutting edge of the research will probably be working for the companies behind these new technologies, thus posing potential conflict-of-interest problems for states wishing to subcontract scientific knowledge.

Indeed, the rapid expansion of scientific knowledge has already overwhelmed regulators at the national level in the world's leading industrialized countries:

- In Canada and France, the blood supply was contaminated because officials failed to have in place a technology policy.

- In the UK, mad cow disease entered the food supply because government scientists were unable to keep up with advances in our understanding of bioforms.

- In Northern Europe, diotoxins contaminated the food supply because Belgian politicians failed to follow up on available knowledge on the eve of an election.

The broad public goods arguments have now also gotten mixed up with national sovereignty issues. A state's sovereign right to decide for itself the best way to protect public health remains a sacrosanct part of the world trading system, upheld unconditionally in the latest global trade agreement. Yet the dismal truth is that with the present dynamic advance in scientific knowledge and new applications, nation-states are no longer competent individually to perform this task. The current country-by-country approach simply bottles up innovation and prevents a great deal of new technology from seeing the light of day promptly. The mix of protectionism, politics and national claims to competence has shown itself to be counter-productive within three years of the WTO signing. So serious has this become, Europe and now North America are desperately trying to re-establish public confidence in the food supply, caused by public fears of biotechnology and the mismanagement of national risk assessment machinery.

Yet government can't just shut down technological advance. Its promise is too great. Millions of afflicted people desperately need new therapies. Cost savings from breakthrough medical technologies based on genomics hold the prospect of a significant health-care dividend. Savings in administrative overheads from the more widespread and coordinated uses of information technology hold the promise of another. For example, the creation and sharing of huge medical databases will allow doctors to make better diagnoses and prescribe more effective treatments. It will also allow health-care managers to be more flexible in their approach to novelty in assessing the cost-effectiveness of treatments. This will enable more varieties of treatments to be prescribed. The tailoring of therapies to genetic profiles will also boost effectiveness dramatically for many patients.

Besides scientific products, there's the issue of the state's continuing ability to manage and maintain complex high-tech infrastructure, such as the air traffic control system or to develop and maintain a smart highway system. The air traffic control system in the US, according to official reports, is about two minutes away from collapse. In Europe, the system has already broken down; arrival and departure delays are just part of daily life. Yet each delay costs airlines thousand of dollars a flight. Congestion in the system means that new flights and new carriers, which would add to competition, cannot be handled. The delays in the system also reduce the profitability of current carriers, which retards their ability to upgrade aging airline fleets around the world.

A new approach to policy making is required; luckily, there are signs that technological help is on the way, in the form of 'ambient computing environments.'

Ambient Computing

In the imminent world of ambient computing, machines will converse with each other regularly—even continuously. Just as our computers now remind us when we need to organize our files and acquire software upgrades (which they will obtain and install with our mouse-click permission), machines in an ambient computing environment will continuously run diagnostics and repairs. Airplanes will substantially organize their own maintenance, as will other vehicles and complicated equipment. Residential housing will have security, smoke detectors and even health monitoring capabilities, linked directly to police, fire departments and medical services. Indeed, many safety and environmental problems we now face are caused by dumb technology that can't modify itself and lacks insight into its own health and well-being.

Ambient computing will change all that. We'll get the public goods of increased safety and reliability as well as sound environmental policy, but the machines themselves will supply it. Government won't have to supply public goods in the form of programs—only rules and objectives. If my fridge is unreliable, it will be obvious from its internal diagnostics; the supplier will fix it or lose me as a customer. If the supplier's subsequent disposal of the fridge is environmentally unsound, the disposal supplier will know it immediately, as well as who is responsible. As for public health issues, in ambient computing environments, domestic waste disposal systems will be able to analyze household and human waste products for any signs of emerging health problems. There will be a unique solution for every problem.

Changing Relationship of Citizen and Government

When the welfare state was originally designed, the power to make decisions was centralized in the hands of Cabinet Ministers (Canada, Europe) and Congressional leaders (Washington). Those who determined the rules of the welfare state generally didn't include more than a handful of the actual recipients of social programs. More present were 'experts' purporting to speak for them, such as trade unionists, university-based sociologists, and politically oriented intellectuals. These groups tended to cluster in political parties with identifiable ideologies. This was true even in the US, where party structure (compared with that of Canada and Europe) is vastly more inclusive and fragmentary—with consequently greater scope for 'political entrepreneurship' no matter which party is in power.

Political parties were the main channels of political information and integration of the voter into the political process. They succeeded to a large extent because political parties delivered informal social services to their supporters. If your kids needed a summer job, if an elderly woman needed her apartment painted, if you needed a ride to the polls, the party (or in the US case, the Party Machine) was there to help. In many countries it was not uncommon for political parties to organize children into youth wings—many young people got their first taste of idealistic politics in Catholic Action, Young Liberals, Young Conservatives, etc.

This broad-based, but concentrated representation on social programs reflected the information costs of participation. In practical terms, for most working people it's worth taking a day off work if (a) you can afford the loss of income and (b) by so doing you may actually receive more income or equivalent benefit. That might happen for doctors, drug company reps, social workers, executive branch officials and trade union leaders. More ordinary people would genuinely doubt their ability to affect any issue. Indeed, many ordinary citizens are not much persuaded of the usefulness of speaking to power on any subject. In Canada, as in Europe, public policy inputs in the modern state are generally restricted to more or less professional policy people. Not participating, not paying attention and not voting on public policy issues is rational in that for most people, time and effort spent in political participation seems unrelated to the alternative prices you could get for doing something else. Accordingly, voters are rational if they strictly limit the time they spend on politics.

Information societies go a long way toward eliminating this problem. The broad implication of these technological changes is the effect on the relationship between the government and the citizen. Matters that are now concerns of public policy will be reconfigured as matters of private concern. The table below is an attempt to show how the 'solution space' has shifted in a number of policy areas from government services to the Net. The table shows a change in the class of information the system feeds on and consequently where a solution is to be found. What constitutes policy at the national level in an industrial society translates into a personal need with a private Net-based solution in an information society.

Table 7.1 Policy from State Perspective to Personal Concerns		
State Policy	**Personal Policy**	**Solution**
Employment rate	Need a job	Personal network
Income distribution	Adequate revenue	Added value (education)
Education levels	Learning access	On-line courses
Health care	Wellness	On-line health monitoring
Crime rates	Personal safety	Alarms and community alternatives to crime
Housing	Home	Community action

As we move forward, the new information society will produce a lot more information at the micro level, and the transaction partners at the micro level will be able to improve outcomes themselves. This is a consequence of ambient computing. Instead of public expectation that government has to make a new law, there will be public expectation that its supplier has to make a new machine. If I need a job, I will use a personalized search engine (called a 'bot, short for a search robot) or I will get an agent to find some alternatives. I, or someone in the help industry, will have a pre-programmed job-bot look over the Web sites with openings suitable for me, and a finance-bot to look for partnering opportunities with entrepreneurs willing to help my business evolve. Maybe there will be an auction-bot to check out where I can sell stuff quick if I need ready cash. In other words, whatever information I need to help me make my own solution will be available to me.[xxxviii]

The impact of this vast increase of information at the micro level will be to change the focus on redistribution that lies at the heart of the governance model in industrial-age states. For the fact is, practical policy analysis focuses less on the pure public goods models than on the distribution of costs and benefits that accompany programs supplying government serv- ices. For example, any tax-funded program costs the rich minority more than the rest of the tax base because they pay higher taxes. So a publicly funded, universal education program creates a benefit for the more numerous average taxpayers at the expense of the less numerous rich—and could thus be expected to win more votes than it would lose.

Or, in contrast, regulated industries often benefit at the expense of the tax- payers. That's because classic regulation limits competition and allows incumbents to set higher prices for a predetermined set of services. These were the models (in many cases still are) that supported local TV cable company monopolies, trucking regulation, financial services regulation; industry models that only began to change in the 1980s. A great many industries developed into informal, regulated cartels before the waves of deregulation. Some continue still.

Most of this regulation was justified in terms of the non-excludable public benefits of health, safety, reliability of service, etc. that supposedly flowed from command-and-control public policy. But even now, that approach is giving way as much as possible before so-called market-based alternatives. For example: companies that clean up the environment find it hard to compete with those that don't. But pollution tax credits change that: they lead to innovative solutions that companies can use and then sell the resulting tax credit to their less advanced competitors. There is even a pol- lution tax-credit-based exchange (the Chicago Board of Trade).

The criticism that this approach creates a license to pollute is spurious. Unlike command-and-control regulation, pollution tax credits create inducements to lessen pollution and build in a transition mechanism that raises the costs of older plants while rewarding those who clean up operations at a rate faster than the law prescribes. The information-rich take on this is that companies with different facilities networked together can figure out how best to combine production cost savings and pollution clean-up using appropriate software.

The policy trend when micro-information abounds will be toward self-enforcing transactions run by competitively supplied machines themselves. This will encourage competition and move us away from government policy based on income redistribution. The role of government in these instances will become that of a network systems administrator, one actor among many, not a unique supplier of jointly consumed services. Instead of tax and transfer systems, we have to look toward networks for the new shape of policy.

The new state will be better able to operate under the conditions of globalization and the interconnectedness of the Net. These governments will be more comfortable without monopolies over social programs at home and abroad. They'll concentrate on making rules that enable people to self-organize to accomplish social aims. Social programs will be designed and delivered in communication and policy loops that involve customers, suppliers and other interested parties, all operating in their citizenship role. Most governments already operate to some extent like this already. Canada has its Canadian Policy Research Networks that regularly contribute to government policy development; the EU has its Forward Policy Unit that draws on outside experts. The US system has always been open to outside policy analysis. Formally or informally, governments are going outside traditional loops for policy strategy as well as fine-tuning and implementing. Gradually, however, this information sharing and consultative activity at the governmental level will diminish as private networks need governments less and interconnected machines take up the burden of keeping our systems operating effectively.

Evolution and Governance

Institutions are supposed to make it easier to do things—reduce transaction costs, in the jargon of economics. When transaction costs are too high—costs such as danger, or uncertainty, or organizing many diverse factions—then many transactions that would otherwise be beneficial will not occur. To get around these things, societies create institutions that reduce dangers, improve predictability and make organization easier. They do this by developing concepts such as property rights and human rights, through a capacity to make and enforce laws, and through systems of accessible and transparent dispute resolution. Institutions and forms of government evolve. History shows this is rarely a smooth process.

However, there are examples of relatively smooth evolution. The emergence of the system of Merchants Law in the Middle Ages—a kind of private law for contract enforcement among traders—was one response to the need for institutions that public policy at the time could not provide. Another example: credit reporting is still a private activity and enforcement of contracts was only incorporated into civil law as national bureaucracies began to extend their grasp in the early modern period. British constitutional history that we learned in school (at least 19th and 20th century constitutional history) is another example of a peaceful transition from a power structure based on land tenure to one based on commercial success.

Today, the world is faced with making another transition—from economies that were modeled on industrial machines to linked economies that behave like biological systems, able to evolve by themselves in response to new stimuli. As our technology generates increasing amounts of economic and transactional information at the micro level, the ability of government to process that information centrally and then develop applicable rules becomes overwhelmed. There is just too much information, changing too quickly, for it to be centrally processed. There is also too much regional variation in a global economy for even sub-units at the nation-state level to fix appropriate solutions for any period of time. Attempting to co-ordinate adjustment from the center can even lead to worse results and de-stabilize national systems as a result—for example when central banks continue to defend official exchange rates long after economic imbalances make that impossible.

Like previous examples of transition, our ways of making public policy have reached a point where they can no longer continue as they are. Unlike other eras, however, there are no real identifiable champions of a particular approach to moving things forward. There is no apparent George Washington, no Robert Peel, no Lords Beveridge or Keynes with a model of government for the information age. But looking for such figures is perhaps mistaken. We live in an age where the necessary information is much more widely distributed, and where many people seem to contribute to solutions every day through new products and services. The process of change we're undergoing is different from that of the past: in place of a few great figures, there are many less conspicuous figures moving forward in their own way. Like the millions of ordinary people who filled in and opened up the Great Plains of North America, there are millions of people who by their choices and actions add a little bit every day to the new reality of an information age. The Great Barrier coral reef has no architect, yet it is a magnificent environment for nature's display, composed of a myriad of interacting, sophisticated sensitive biological systems. As our society becomes more cybernetic, our need for overall architects and universal monarchs will also diminish—as indeed our civil processes change so that those with such ambitions find other outlets, such as business and the arts. New, positive social processes and technological innovations will crowd out policy expressed in the form of government programs.

Chapter 8

Reconfiguring the State

"Opportunity is missed by most people because it is dressed in overalls and looks like work"

—Thomas Edison

The challenge of adjusting the state to the impact of a global information economy is big. But it can be managed. To see how, we need one or two more ideas to add to those of de-territorialization, dis-intermediation, and policy mortality discussed earlier. We need to understand the distinction between *political* capacity and *policy* capacity.

Political Capacity and Policy Capacity

Why are the governments in some countries so much more able than others to bring about the changes needed for countries to modernize? People who study economic development have come up with the idea of political capacity to help explain why. Countries with higher political capacity can raise more money from more people. Somehow, more people in those countries are willing to pay more taxes to their governments in order to attain national development goals. They buy in to what government is trying to do. Political scientists don't talk about political capacity, but say that 'government performance' yields a similar result. For example, Arend Lijphart, in *Patterns of Democracy* (1999,Yale), concludes that "consensus democracy" leads to "kinder, gentler" societies. In other words, systems that ensure more diverse representation in government lead to policies that balance income redistribution and productivity goals better than do 'majority take all' or 'first pass the post' systems, such as those in Britain, Canada and the US. The idea of political capacity and government performance are both strongly linked to government as the central economic actor and distribution agent.

Redesigning Government

It's exactly this aspect of government performance that is most directly challenged by the move to the Internet. Other things remaining equal, it can no longer be taken for granted that national governments will have the capacity to play this central socio-economic role. But while the transfer of a critical level of economic activity to the Internet will weaken the *policy* capacity of government, it may not necessarily weaken government's *political* capacity. The distinction is crucial, although it is a difficult one to make and any separation in fact is probably impossible. In chapters 2 and 3 we touched on the distinction. When welfare-state governments were unable to control spending or to eliminate inflation, public trust and approval of government declined. This trend, combined with the capabilities offered by new information technology, produced a shift of the electorate's own policy framework from macro to micro perspectives. People now define problems in more personal terms and seek more personal solutions: government has become perceived as more of a problem than a solution in the lives of most ordinary voters. Declines in *policy* capacity generate declines in *political* capacity.

No wonder, then, that one response of governments around the world to the new technologies is to devise programs to re-invent government. Some of these include ways to offer government information and services 24/7 using the Net as a backbone for this added convenience. This is a design for improving the service-delivery component of government policy.[xxxix]

Other approaches have focused on using the new technologies to strengthen popular participation in government—through such devices as on-line voting and on-line town meetings. These are attempts to strengthen government's political capacity to appeal to more people and to popularize policy by taking back some of the policy-making from the economists and other specialists. Two points about these efforts: first, they show how difficult it is to divorce politics and policy; and second, they are essentially ways of shoring up the current idea of the state as the chief economic distributor.

Embeddedness

Trying to preserve the way things are done is a flawed strategy because it is fighting against a logic embedded in the new technology itself—a logic that kicks away the props of the old system. The old system existed because government could enforce its territorial boundaries, had superior information gathering and processing capabilities, and had unlimited taxation capacity. None of those props can continue to support government in its central role—they've been swept away by the Net. The notion of *embeddedness* goes back to Karl Polyani[xl] who, during the 1940s, argued powerfully against laissez-faire capitalism. He said it was an elegant but unworkable theoretical ideal—unworkable because in real life there were too many social claims embedded in the economy. These included claims of custom (such as family responsibilities, ties of emotion, and traditional concepts of fairness and justice) that made models based on 'rational, maximizing behavior' very limited in application. People generally do not try to maximize, so markets are always more or less inefficient and thus more or less unstable. Government, therefore, had a fundamental role as a compensating device. But these compensators are now also embedded in the new technology, in the gift culture of the Net.

Figure 8.1   Financial Times Online

FT.com
FINANCIAL TIMES

NEWS & ANALYSIS/WORLD

Hague takes leaf out of Bush's book
By Robert Shrimsley, Chief Political Correspondent
Published: June 21, 2000 19:42 GMT / Last updated: June 21, 2000 21:29 GMT

Plans to change the tax treatment of charities to encourage them to take a more
Active role in welfare provision are being studied by the Tories as a possible
Manifesto commitment.

Among the areas being studied are exemption from value added tax, a reduction in
Bureaucracy over tax deductibility of charitable donations and reform of the Charity
Commissioners.

William Hague discussed the idea yesterday with two policy advisors to George W.
Bush, the Republican candidate for US president...

Adaptation to this new reality may be difficult because doing so means
making some distinction between policy and politics. Policy is being
stripped from government and is now to be found on the Net. All the elements are there, from information to advocacy to the tools for implementation. To be sure, it is not all pulled together in the way government
presently does it. The new civil society, which has made such good use of
the organizational capacities of the Net, has yet to learn how to handle
social policy delivery. But there are signs are that it is occurring, somewhat
under protest, as governments download increasing responsibility onto
civil society.

There is now far more extensive policy-oriented discussion about poverty
and the excluded, discussion that involves more people than ever before,

more money to deal with the problems as a result of the economic growth of the 'long boom.' There is even a dawning realization that perhaps government's role is not to get directly involved but to develop rules that make it easier and more affordable for people to help their neighbors.

Technology Fixes

There's another class of social problems, arising from our extensive inventory and use of 'dumb' machines, that the new technology can address directly. The role of government may well be to encourage such changes through legislation, not programs. For example, the technology exists to make guns that only their owners can fire: illegally obtained weapons simply won't work. Cars can be manufactured that won't start if the driver can't pass a breathalyzer test. Machines are being built that can self diagnose and report problems. Potentially damaging chemicals can be tagged so that they are immediately identifiable and traceable. As well, smart toilets and electronic health workers can produce early warnings of health problems and send the results to a health professional. Together with other forms of tele-medicine, this will slash the costs of health care while raising standards of service.

Some of this is already commercially available, more of it is on the drawing boards of major companies, and some of it is creeping into law. A vastly important area concerns digital cash. On-line e-money is more reliable, can't be stolen and can be carried in electronic portfolios to eliminate the risk of losses from fluctuating foreign exchange rates. Real-time settlement of payments would eliminate bounced checks and reduce costs by reducing the amount of money floating between transactions (perhaps 7 to 10 per cent of global business revenues). Technology itself can therefore go some distance to reducing the need for government policy capacity.

At the same time, however, enhanced government 'political capacity' is crucial to realizing the benefits of technology. Take the issue of organized crime and the impact of electronic cash. Would electronic cash reduce or enhance criminal money laundering? The answer would depend on whether people would support limited programs of payment identification. Governments that could win public trust would be able to do this.

Competition Between Jurisdictions

The importance of trust takes us to another element of the argument, that of jurisdictional competition. Taxpayers everywhere want to organize their affairs so that their tax payments equal the value of services they believe they're getting back. As this becomes easier to do, more people will do it and competition for tax revenue will increase between jurisdictions. Governments may compete by using their tax systems to try to improve the revenue-gathering potential for their tax base. Indeed, such competition exists now and it's quite fierce in North America. Governments regularly make deals with business, for example, reducing an immediate tax burden for the promise of more direct investment in a specific area within a specified period of time.

In the competition we're describing, one strategy might well be to set personal taxes slightly below current levels, aiming at broadening the tax base (and thus raising revenues). Other government strategies might set high income tax rates above a certain income threshold with a view to attracting a broader base at lower tax levels. Some jurisdictions might allow people to negotiate their own taxes—lowering income tax in favor of the sales tax take from an agreed-upon level of local spending. Swiss cantons already employ this strategy for affluent new residents. States might negotiate similar packages, taking into account volunteer activity. One of the few unfailingly reliable propositions in economics is that competition brings along a lot more supply with a lot better value for consumers. The new technologies that inject consumer competition into government activity will have this effect if governments can innovate and compete without losing political capacity.

So far we've argued that governments will generally choose to stop supply-ing services in favor of setting up frameworks of law and self-enforcing regulation (such as certified compliance programs) to ensure the standards of service supply. Suppose, however, governments continue to supply some services. This raises the possibility that such services could trade across borders.

Trade in Government Services

Trade in government services is already present to a limited extent in world trade agreements, and up for improvement in the next round of trade talks. Generally it affects government procurement of goods and services from private suppliers; i.e., the government as customer. Countries have struggled to keep social services and education off the trade table. But these positions are unsustainable from an economic point of view, even if negotiators may continue to resist trade liberalization in this area. Even now governments lack the resources to reverse the decline of whole chunks of the state-supplied education and Medicare systems. Free trade in these services would open doors to alternative suppliers whose competition would promote innovation and keep costs down.

In the North American context, it seems likely that post-secondary edu-cation will see free trade first. Competition with US universities and graduate schools has always been part of the Canadian landscape, and their on-line arrival will not make that much difference to Canadian thinking. The difference is that under NAFTA, virtual presence gives entities the right to national treatment, and under current funding arrangements, provincial governments would find themselves shelling out subsidies to anyone who qualified as a university. The only viable solutions would be to eliminate the payments altogether or to pay stu-dents directly and let them decide among all the suppliers. This would be a generally beneficial change—access to the US student market would more than make up for any Canadian students Canadian universities lost, and access to US alternative programs would broaden the range of available programs in Canada.

Likely far more controversial would be free trade in health services. Canada's tax-funded health-care services provide universal access to treatment for all Canadian residents. The plans are organized on a single-payer basis by provincial governments. There are few cross-border provisions, but within limits, the plans cover residents in Canada outside their province, although additional private coverage is necessary outside Canada. The quality of service is uneven, and the outlook is not good, as an aging population will add stress to an already overloaded system. Local politics, labor relations and a number of other issues make it difficult to reorganize services as profoundly as some doctors believe necessary.

Free trade in health services, combined with the ability (conferred by on-line business) to allocate virtual employment around the continent, would be an improvement for all stakeholders. Within a North American context, it would allow the two demands—low taxes/expensive services or high taxes/ affordable service—to find their own supply. Those who like US tax levels and would be content with the assurance of US-style benefits would opt for that formula. Those who prefer the Canadian model could opt for that—and become eligible for Canadian benefits. Many of these could be delivered on-line or with on-line mediation (for example, Canadian/US drugs or diagnostic services). Physical service delivery could be supplied locally too, using franchised suppliers outside the home jurisdiction. Canadian-scheme hospitals could operate in the US next to American ones and vice versa. Customers could opt for the schemes they prefer.

In fact, this sort of thing already happens in a limited away along the northern US border (in southern Quebec, for example, medical doctors who have been downsized out of Canadian Medicare have thriving businesses made up of Americans. Nurses who have been downsized out of Canadian hospitals find lucrative work in American hospitals just 10 miles further down the road. Across the country, US oldsters come to Canada to fill their drug prescriptions at less cost.)[xli] Expanding market access rules would simply extend the rights of those not favored by proximity. The big advantage to Canada would be the additional revenue from US clients (assuming the feasibility of appropriate screening, etc.) and the reduction in claims from Canadian patients who preferred the benefits of US treatment (faster service, better technology). On a more general level, the recent World Health Organization survey of health care showed enormous variations in performance quality, even among advanced countries. Although the WHO took no position on this, clearly trade is the easiest way to arbitrage away the differences and raise the levels of access to improved quality.[xlii]

Think of a health-care establishment as a bundle of specialized competencies. Pharmacy, data and informatics management, maintenance and janitorial, accounting and financial management, human resources, public relations, specialized waste disposal—an enormous range of disciplines and skills. A great many of these, such as data and informatics, waste disposal, janitorial services, can now be supplied by multinationals on contract to health-care organizations. As well, all the pharmaceutical products used in medical treatment come one way or another from multinational companies. In the final analysis, there is no reason why the medical professionals themselves could not also be supplied in this manner. Indeed, this already occurs in global disaster relief through such voluntary organizations as Doctors without Borders. In a world in which scarce professional talent is perhaps the most valuable resource of all, cross-border organization by franchise or by direct supply of needed competencies offers the promise of substantial efficiency and welfare gains. Conversely, blocking such developments virtually guarantees less beneficial outcomes.

Program Financing v Government Financing

Another aspect of government reconfiguration is the shift from government financing to self-financing of programs. Many governments, especially high-tax ones, have opted to target program benefits rather than organize on a universal basis. In practice, this means that many program benefits are taxed back from those whose incomes exceed a predetermined threshold. For example, if child tax credits or old age security payments are universal, but are taxed back from households with incomes above a certain level, that 'clawed-back' money is recycled to pay for the programs that go to the targeted groups. Thus, in such countries, a part of virtually all social program spending is self-financed. These are significant changes. But more changes could be made to squeeze more advantage out of the way governments finance such programs. They could 'securitize' the programs.

Governments now raise money for all programs all at once, by selling bonds. They also try to stagger their borrowing to balance short-term and long-term requirements with bonds of different maturities—say 5, 10 and 25 or 30 years. The bond prices reflect expectations of inflation as well as the government's ability to finance itself over all. (They also help keep capital markets liquid.) Yet there are some programs—typically operated by such government agencies as automobile insurance (Canadian provinces) and low cost mortgages (US Fannie Mae) that are securitized. In other words, the streams of money in these insurance policy and mortgage payments are used to guarantee low risk investment vehicles (securities) like certificates of deposit.

Investors who want to invest in mortgages can buy a certificate of deposit from a mortgage lender (the government is the biggest mortgage lender.) The certificate works like a bond: for the price of the bond, the investor gets a steady income stream plus the return of her capital. This securitizing principle could also to be extended to social programs. If an ongoing program is already 80 per cent self-sustaining, it could lessen still further its costs by packaging the tax claw-back and using it to guarantee low-risk investment certificates. The money received from purchasers of the certificates could be used to offset net outflows on the non-self-funding program elements. As a deposit, it would attract interest. Or, it could be directly applied to, say, capital expenditures.

Operating this way would avoid the effects of deficit financing at the macro-economic level—that is, it would reduce the government's annual net borrowing requirement. It would also solve a major problem in government finance that the private sector solved more than a decade ago—that of risk distribution. Basically, it would take government out of the business of assuming risks of social programs and pass them directly onto the program investors.

Mental Models: The Hardest Nut

The Keynesian welfare state always assumed that the policy capacity of governments would eventually trump the political capacity. Like the Bible's seven fat years, seven lean years cycle, the welfare state would harvest tax surpluses in good years to spend in bad years, shoring up the system to ward off a 1930s-style collapse. It would achieve this bliss because the system itself was enclosed within the boundaries of the national state. International borrowing and lending were restricted by capital controls. Because taxpayers held the debt they would have to pay off, the system was supposedly self-stabilizing. The supply of funds for investment always equaled the supply for saving and the amount spent on consumption controlled total demand for goods and services.

If people preferred to save rather than consume, interest rates would fall, new projects would emerge to soak up the new investment, jobs and incomes would increase. If consumption rose too fast, interest rates would rise as savings became tight, unemployment would rise as interest-rate-sensitive sectors like housing and consumer durables slowed, consumption would drop off, and the cycle could begin again. The role of government in this circular flow between consumption and saving or investment was to stabilize the system if necessary. Governments did this by using the tax system to fine tune demand, spending or cutting taxes as the economy slowed and raising taxes to dampen demand in booms.

In this model, governments would always have the political capacity to insist on the economically necessary policy. If policy demanded higher unemployment, well then, there was unemployment insurance to take away the sting and the policy levers would be effective enough that any fluctuations would be brief.

Even though the reality was a bit different, economists kept this model alive for at least 20 years after World War II and did not change it much when the Bretton Woods Accords collapsed and the US dollar went off the gold standard in 1971. The liberalization of capital markets broke the equality relationship between savings and investment at the national level. Whatever policy measures a government took were discounted against the range of government policy around the world. Money goes where it's best treated. Capital would flow from falling markets into rising markets. In this context, Keynesian levers could be harmful: the Keynesian prescription for say, inflation, would be higher taxes to curb consumer and producer demand. In the context of open capital markets, this policy would simply cause higher unemployment and higher government spending on income-support programs, leading to higher government borrowing and larger deficits. A strict dedication to steady price levels through tough monetary policy, not Keynesian demand management, proved the optimal policy choice.

It took governments most of the 1970s and half of the 1980s to figure out that the rules had changed. Governments leaped into world capital markets as a way to borrow off- shore what they couldn't raise at home, in order to offer programs to voters at what amounted to below-market prices. Debts rose to finance the difference between programs and taxes to the point that debt-servicing costs outweighed program costs. At this point, the world's lenders drew a line. Whereas under Keynesian concepts, economic policy was supposed to trump politics by force of reason, now economic policy trumped politics by something akin to *force majeure*. Capital must have its way.

One result of this has been to weaken the national state in both its policy and political capacities and raise questions of legitimacy: property (in the form of loans) suddenly imposed its imperatives on politics (in the form of social programs and government spending). By what right did bondholders, many of whom were off-shore, start telling elected governments what to do politically?

The answer is subtle: there is a clear interdependence between a government's ability to make and deliver effective policy—its policy capacity—and a government's ability to win public support and general commitment to a set of politically determined priorities—its political capacity. Where the policy and political capacities overlap and are coherent, the state itself is legitimate and will be able to function effectively. But where politics and policy get out of synch and begin acting at cross-purposes, conflict will result; ultimately the state will lose its legitimacy through its failure to resolve those conflicts.

The postwar shift to a Keynesian welfare state was legitimate as long as the policy capacity and political capacities of the state remained aligned. The public borrowing sprees on international capital markets in the last quarter of the 20th century broke that alignment. Now the emergence of a global economy, operating across a single Internet-linked web, has changed the rules again. The new environment supplies government with different and unfamiliar tools to ensure its policy/political coherence—and takes away those the state has become most accustomed to using.

The challenge now is to rearrange our expectations of government—and our expectations of ourselves—so that the new alignment can be made to work. An important element in this realignment is the redistribution of risk. As individual citizens, we are increasingly taking on risk that the state and other private organizations used to assume. It is therefore more essential that we align our actions to take this into account. One advantage of this shift in political and policy capacity, an aspect we have only touched upon up to now, is that the character of politics can now be significantly enhanced.

The Challenge of Freedom

Ancient Greek philosophers regarded politics as man's highest, noblest achievement. The ability to organize into city-states and establish conditions for advancing humanity seemed to them the essence of being human. A key element of those conditions was the requirement of citizens to participate in political life. Service was compulsory and elections ran like jury duty: the assembly was selected by lot and sat briefly. City leaders were chosen when the assembly approved their programs.

Underpinning this willingness to serve as a public official was a conviction that the political life of the *polis* defined what it was to be human. The *polis* gave status and opportunity for achievement in the eyes of fellow citizens. This approach to government was held to be uniquely western.

It's a leap from ancient Athens to today. In the intervening millennia, our societies have moved from a world of small settlements and town meetings to robust representative democracies, to today's large, self-absorbed government bureaucracies. As these central governments have grown more powerful, our prosperity has increased, and the collective achievements accomplished have surpassed those of any other time. Great hospitals and universities, spectacularly capable business corporations have each in their own way propelled us to the most technologically sophisticated civilization in history. But at the same time, our sense of humanity seems under assault, if not diminished.

The challenge to the state posed by the global information economy offers an opportunity to insert ourselves as human beings back into the policy/political capacity equation. A global system of distributed knowledge, organized along co-operative pathways, enables the people of the planet to come together at any level they wish. This is not an advocacy of violence. Quite the reverse: it is a signpost to a newly important area of global politics—what some writers have called the Noosphere[xliii]—the realm of ideas. The information economy shortens the distance between ideas and practice to near zero. The new civil society that has developed along the information pathways offers some impressive approaches to bringing public concerns into expert debates. The opportunity and the challenge we face is to use such tools and techniques, and to develop more of them as needed, to bring into convergence both the policy and political capacities of our collective organizations.

The challenge of freedom is actually to take the power that freedom gives us and use it constructively. If we don't feel equal to the task, we can take comfort in the fact that historically, no one ever has. This time the task will be especially difficult because so many givens of an earlier era are in the process of change. But the task is also easier because the process of rising returns is so much more accessible. New norms and standards of practice can prevail simply through widespread general acceptance.

Orwellian Threats

There are other, less happy outcomes possible. Governments could shift the process of transformation to an information economy into reverse almost invisibly, especially if appropriate political conditions arose or the long boom came to an unexpected early demise. A sample scenario:

- Step One: The state inserts itself into the development and promotion of the new technologies, careful to use metaphors that cloud the real interconnectedness and leveling impact of them. (For example, the metaphor of the electronic highway, or Infobahn, suggests the world of cyberspace is a road one travels along. This is not correct. The Infocosm or Web is a place of simultaneous action, where people can do things without the barriers of time and space.) In promoting the Information Highway, the state learns to maximize its power to aggregate information and to maintain a powerful symbolic presence before its citizens. This obscures the fact that the Infocosm is a virtual presence that is replacing governments' physical presence as they withdraw from program activity.

- Step Two. The state declares war on social deviance. Cocaine and marijuana use are demonized, and risks of terrorism are highlighted by security agencies in pursuit of broader powers and more resources. At the same time, really big crime joins the global economy as a full participant. Parliaments and legislatures find themselves helpless rubber-stampers before the Executive Branch all over the West. Politics itself becomes criminalized as political debate is reduced to public trials of incumbent officials through news leaks to the media. Moreover, all of the above discourages intelligent discussion about sensible alternatives to the current bankrupt and dangerous state structure.

- Step Three. Security agencies successfully obtain expanded surveillance powers, allegedly to crush terrorism and drug trafficking. In fact, the new powers are to be used to crack down on tax evasion. The aim is to terrify self-employed middle-class people who cannot afford a rumble with the system; they will simply not try to take full advantage of the globalizing tax system. (The US National Security Agency subjects to surveillance all US–foreign telecom traffic; to the NSA, the traffic is an open book, e-mail becomes an open letter. The FBI's Carnivore program reads mail on the sites of co-operative Internet Service Providers. The new UK snoop bill, the Regulation of Investigatory Powers Act, includes an obligation to divulge cryptography keys to investigators.)

- Step Four. In the guise of increasing the access of information have-nots and to promote universal access to the Internet—perhaps also including a mercantilist appeal to 'national' portals rather than American ones—governments begin issuing plastic access cards to households. Eventually these plastic cards are upgraded to include a microchip designed to check an individual's tax account whenever he or she tries to log on to the system. An extension of this technology will permit a sweep of taxpayers' bank accounts on a regular basis based on their tax due dates. The privacy (or lack of privacy) implications of the new technology will become so thoroughly embedded in the public mind that the Internet goes the way of television and CB-Radio. People only use it when necessary for specific purposes, like an ATM terminal.

- Step Five. State officials everywhere breathe a sigh of relief and get down to the serious business of running countries and regions again. Economic depression is explained away as an inevitable result of an inherently unstable global financial system, soon to be replaced by capital controls, fixed exchange rates and Keynesian economic programs.

This alternative scenario sounds paranoid, even to us, mainly because governments are not so smart that they can program such things from an initial starting point. But people in government are paid to capitalize on developments, and that is all this five-step solution requires. A simple algorithm saying "capitalize on this step to increase power in the next" will do it.

The private sector represents a similar threat. Just like governments, on-line merchandisers have the technology to read employees' e-mail and to see what Web sites you visit. An American Management Association study shows that 54 per cent of US companies oversee their employees' Internet use and 38 per cent store and review employees' e-mail.[xliv] The sale of databases with critical identifiers in them (such as drivers' licenses, social insurance numbers and credit card information) makes it relatively easy for organized and knowledgeable criminals to steal identities. The technology marketers use to identify and track the habits of consumers can also be used to accumulate personal information which, when assembled, amounts to an invasion of privacy. Proclaimed privacy policies by reputable companies are not audited and, should the company be wound up, may not survive the company. Databases are assets that can be sold for funds to satisfy creditors. Computers on networks are also too often vulnerable to outside hacking and surveillance.

Now, to be sure, one difference between state surveillance and employer supervision is that companies work by contract with individuals. These contracts can be negotiated and enforced by the parties involved, whereas the political process essentially controls the contract between government and citizens. The failure to build privacy protection into the network reflects the needs of marketers and law enforcement interests over the rights of individuals. The surveillance capabilities of the Net are at odds with the architecture of confidence required to make the Internet a successful technology. Yet the solution is also at hand: the evolution of ubiquitous encryption to even the balance between individuals and powerful organizations. Already, a number of sites and products exist to provide various levels of defense against outside attacks, from firewalls to 'anonymizers' to serious, industrial-strength encryption programs. As public confidence in network confidentiality plummets, the market for such technical solutions will grow. Ultimately they will become standard equipment on all network devices, whether governments like it or not. People have the right to control the information about themselves that other people obtain, and will insist upon its proper exercise.

Without information technology, humankind cannot take the next step towards expanding the boundaries of civilization so that democracy and non-discrimination among nations can become the hallmarks of the way global society operates. But only a vigilant citizenry can ensure that it happens.

#

PART THREE

No Small Change

Chapter 9

Mastering Change

"The failure of nerve occurs when even given all the relevant facts, the would-be prophet cannot see that they point to an inescapable conclusion."

—Arthur C. Clarke, Profiles of the Future

The shift of human activity from physical space to cyberspace is now not only established but has as many profound implications as any past changes humanity has experienced. Technologically speaking, the electronic equivalent of the industrial revolution—the digital revolution—is now more or less accomplished. Western civilization has already experienced the technological shift from industrial economies (in which wealth creation was based on the transformation of raw materials) to the digital economy (in which wealth creation is based on the transformation of information). We are now in the midst of the accompanying *social transformation*. Not only is the way business is done being transformed, so are political structures based on sovereign nation-states. The question now facing us is to what extent, if any, can the nation state adapt to these changes. The state has many functions that it can still perform well. But its earlier predominant role in social policy is a spent force. Our best hope in this arena lies with the new civil society in which the state will be one voice among many.

The Impact of Communications

How could communications technologies bring about such profound change? In fact, that's what communications technologies do. Plato recognized that writing would destroy oral culture and its basis in human memory with no additional gain in accuracy, since written texts could be interpreted any which way once no one remembered what their author really had in mind. Harold Innis, a Canadian economist and historian considered by many to be the intellectual godfather of Marshall McLuhan, developed a theory of empires in which communications technology played a decisive enabling role. Innis argued that writing helped the Roman Empire expand, but it also ensured its growing rigidity by encouraging the accumulation of power at the center.

Ease of communication also encouraged the spread of the Eastern mystery religions from the Empire's Asian periphery to its European center. Of these religions, the most powerful came to be Christianity. Ultimately Rome's successor, the Catholic Church responded to Rome's decline by substituting pictures for text and survived as a universal institution when nothing else could—until people learned to read again and to voice their own ideas. This occurred after the discovery of movable type in the first half of the 15th century; it made possible the printing of affordable books and broadsheets. This again changed the balance of power in society. No established authority could withstand the circulation of ideas and the expansion of literacy in the early modern period. Protestantism and reason ultimately vanquished authority and absolutism, aided by an age of print that produced books, newspapers and a literary class that lived by promoting ideas.

Now it's one thing to understand that communications technologies make a difference. It's another to understand why. The argument here is more complex. Students of modern Europe's five centuries of revolutions, like

Professor Charles Tilly, list three main circumstances leading to revolutionary situations. These are (1) when discrepancies arise between what states demand and what they can induce their citizens to perform, (2) when states threaten rights of collective identities of groups of citizens, and (3) when rulers' powers collapse in the presence of rivals.[xlv] All these conditions are now potentially present and will intensify as we move more deeply and extensively onto the Internet. Why? Because as we stressed throughout this book, the Net effectively decouples government from territory, drastically reduces government's role as an intermediary between taxpayers and program recipients, and undermines the most basic economic concepts that underpin a welfare role for the state.

Although these conditions make a revolutionary situation likely, they don't make it inevitable. In fact, understanding the implications may make it easier for us to navigate through this transformation successfully and avoid the costs normally associated with drastic change. Social change does not make disruption inevitable. But when it begins to impact the role of the state, individual rights, and the definition of wealth, the *prospect* of change becomes far more difficult to manage.

As important as any of the forces accelerating change is the notion of what occurs in the very process of change itself. Modern sociologists speak of an identifiable 'break' between the modern (meaning contemporary) and the past. In fact, there have been many such breaks between past and present in the evolution of western society. What they all have in common is that those who lived after the break are different—they share a different mix of social knowledge from those who lived in the past.

Societies built around scientific awareness, such as ours, are very different from those built around, say, religious observance. And, of course, societies built around industrial logic and experience are not the same as those that incarnate the logic of an information society. In a very real sense, the concept of a break between one type of society and another corresponds to the model of change used in our discussion. Our model is based on the proposition that technological change gives new meanings to institutions as it confers new capabilities.

There is no reason to believe that the social changes we are facing are any different from those in the past. There will be a break between those who successfully transition to an information society and its associated halo of new understandings, and those who don't. For those who prefer 'organizational learning' models to those of discontinuous change, the challenge is clear: can organizations, such as national governments, learn sufficiently quickly to get over or through the historical break, or will they become trapped, unable to change, in a world that is rushing by them?

Perestroika and the Collapse of the Soviet Empire

Perhaps no better modern example exists of the folly of rigidly refusing to acknowledge change than the tragedy that befell the people of Central and Eastern Europe. With democracy suppressed under totalitarian rule and economic flexibility destroyed by generations of central planning, the ancient states of Eastern Europe—Poland, Czechoslovakia, Hungary, and their eastern neighbors, Rumania, Moldova, Ukraine and Belarus—found themselves utterly unequipped to support themselves after the fall of Communism. Worse, the former Soviet Union and the Russian people have sunk into kleptocracy. True, for the most part, the revolutions in state control in Eastern Europe were non-violent. But the challenge of re-building those economies is huge. The expansion of Europe to include them in the European Union is itself a daunting challenge to the capacity of the Euro-institutions to manage change. What is instructive for our concerns here is that the states that had the most vigorous black markets under Communism—Hungary and Poland—became the states with the least difficult adjustments. Why? Because the relatively market-oriented black markets encouraged some of the social values needed to succeed in a market economy, such as innovation and entrepreneurship. What was officially condemned in the old order became virtuous in the new. Rarely has a "break" between past and present been clearer.

Maybe because we're told every change is revolutionary (like a 'revolutionary' new hair spray), we tend to think social change is easy. It is not. It is one of the most difficult and dangerous processes imaginable. Changes in the 20th century were no better managed than in the 19th —indeed far worse, if the price is reckoned in total destruction. The crux of the present matter is that the shift to an information society in cyberspace is at least as profound as the earlier shift to an urban industrial society. It represents an historical break equal to any previous transformation. There is no reason to believe that we know how to handle it, or that it will take us any less time to figure out than changes faced by our forebears.

We have to recognize the profundity or scale of the changes underway in order to fully absorb this new way of doing things. We are witnessing the emergence of a new global civil society. The technologies underlying this shift are information technologies. They interconnect and transmit and transform information. They do so on such a scale that they transform our institutions and ways of life. Used properly, they can enhance the human condition. For the first time, by using those technologies, people the world over can be politically free and economically secure at the same time. But even if the goal is clear, the only thing we can be sure about is that the institutional framework for getting there will be very different from what surrounds us now. The new institutions will be at least as different as feudalism was from the ancient world, or national democratic capitalism was from the *ancien régime*.

From that perspective, the astonishing thing is how little has changed in the information-age public sector in contrast to the private sector. Our concepts of work, family, authority, etc. have changed and continue to evolve away from the industrial model. But throughout the western world and Japan, governments cling to pre-information-age models, like children seeking comfort from their favorite blankets. From a practical policy perspective, most governments seem to be treating the change as though it were a new wonder drug or a technology like the automobile. That is, a change embodying profound implications, but embodying little to destabilize the governance model that underlies the foundations of our political systems, and by implication, our ability to resolve social conflicts and set collective goals. That is neither a justifiable view nor a sustainable strategy for dealing with what is one of the most important historical breaks of all time.

A Bit of History

Yet because ours is not the first era to face the challenge of adapting our institutions to profound and dislocating change, history provides some instructive examples. The chief problem, from the standpoint of the state, has been to secure the legitimacy of the new arrangements. One key to this legitimacy lies in maintaining the coherence between policy and political capacity. But how is a state to achieve it?

Nineteenth century Europe achieved it through nationalism. Then, the challenge was to work out a convergence between the principles of a democratic middle-class state and those of monarchy. The French Revolution tried but failed to bring it off. The other European states, inspired by that failure, managed to arrange their affairs to preserve their monarchies. When the 19th passed into the 20th century, France was the only Continental power with a purely republican form of government. Most countries had become constitutional monarchies—with the constitutional part shrinking and autocracy (and along with it poverty) increasing as one moved eastward until the Russian Empire. By 1914, only Russia remained purely and disastrously autocratic on a pre-modern model—with a population that was 90 per cent composed of illiterate peasants living in a condition similar to that of sharecroppers on large, quasi-feudal estates.

Despite the range of solutions, the underlying reconciliations of the middle class state and the monarchical state were all accomplished through reinforcing the same principle—that of nationalism. As we know from history, the militant nationalism of the *second* half of the 19th century ultimately proved fatal to the civilization that supported it, exploding in the catastrophe of World War I. Still, some of those convergences were more successful than others, success revealing itself in terms of economic prosperity. The link between prosperity and successful convergence was no accident. England was—in the eyes of many contemporaries as well as historians—by far the most successful example of how a monarchical state could adjust to a middle-class civilization, to the mutual enhancement of both. There are lessons in that success for us, a century later.

The lesson generally drawn from the British experience was the superiority of 'evolution' over 'revolution.' True, today you could say that as the United States showed, a middle-class revolution that scrapped the monarchy altogether could be even more successful. But at the close of the 19th century, the US was by no means well understood. Its constitution had ultimately failed to engineer a successful convergence between North and South and the resulting civil war had been one of the bloodiest in history. On the world stage, the US was still an untested experiment. Great Britain, in contrast, had last faced the threat of civil war 200 years before and ruled over the largest, most liberal trade area in the world. It was the backstop of a global financial system that ran on a gold standard managed by the Bank of England, and had successfully kept the world free of major war for 85 years.

For ordinary people, the economic success was just as spectacular. The condition of ordinary Britons improved over the course of the century so that, despite the population doubling, general welfare *more* than doubled. Perhaps most significant of all, the growth of national and international markets ended once and for all the specter of famine in the British Isles— a specter that became a horrible reality during Irish famine of the mid-1840s. Behind this achievement lay industrialization, which Britain accomplished first at home and then abroad, financing successful industrial revolutions in North America, France and Germany. What so astonished contemporaries was that Britain came through the historical break of industrialization and the creation of a consumer society without any apparent wrinkle or tear in its institutional fabric.

When one looks a little more closely at British success, an important key is the successful reform of electoral institutions[xlvi] that brought to power a new class of entrepreneurs whose wealth was based on new, previously under-represented, industrial centers like Birmingham and Manchester. The second step in Britain's success was the adoption of Free Trade with the repeal of the Corn Laws a decade or so later. These two steps sealed into place a new power equation that favored the new, factory-based industrial economy over the previous agricultural and financial commercial economy. This change was accompanied by measures that wiped out many of the state's policy instruments: the electoral system that kept the old power structures in place, the system of tariffs that financed the old state. What's more, by introducing free trade that included agricultural products, the measures also wiped out the revenue base of the old landed aristocracy (high returns from protected agriculture). At the same time they reduced the price of food —a major factor in the affordable wage level of the newly forming British working classes.

By the 1850s, the old English state that had lost the American colonies but had established Britain as the leading global power was gone. In its place was an even more effective and competent state—the product of 30 years of continual change that in effect retrofitted British institutions to suit a new industrial economy.

How did Britain do it while continental Europe faced revolution and insurrection over the same agenda? Clearly, the expansion of the franchise expanded the political capacity of the new state, which in turn expanded its policy capacity. But having an expanded policy capacity and knowing how to use it are not automatically the same. Another key difference between England and the great continental powers was that England's economy was a *maritime* economy. Its essential dynamic was global trade across the oceans of the world.

Freedom of the Seas

In the 1840s, the economy was characterized by the exchange of British high-value-added manufactured products for resource-based commodities from around the world. By the 1870s, this developed into financial rents from successful re-investment in industrial enterprises in those overseas commercial partners—whether inside or outside the formal confines of Empire. Key to the successful pursuit of these overseas interests was the concept of 'freedom of the seas.' This concept, still a key feature of maritime law, held that the seas were free of jurisdiction and that ships at sea could ply freely whatever routes they wished. This marked a sharp reversal from the Navigation Acts of the 18th century, which sought to dictate the course of ships at sea in order to control trade flows. Those acts, one of the factors that cost Britain its American colonies, gradually disappeared after the Napoleonic wars, replaced by the freedom of the seas doctrine.

The embrace of free trade linked Britain's economy directly to maritime commerce, governed by the free play of market forces that were in turn underpinned by freedom of the seas. By the 1840s, with the erosion of the Navigation Acts, British ports were open to world shipping on a non-discriminatory basis. This propelled a major rise in national prosperity that confirmed Britain as the richest country in Europe with its highest living standards. Paradoxically from the standpoint of the 18th century, adopting freedom of the seas—and relinquishing the national power to regulate the course of shipping implicit in the Navigation Acts— enhanced Britain's policy capacity. *Less was more.*

The question arises: if Britain abandoned tariffs, with what did it finance its state expenditures? Interestingly, the new industrial class came to power armed with the idea of re-introducing a tax that had hitherto only been used in national emergencies—an income tax. In 1842, Conservative Prime Minister Robert Peel introduced the income tax as a 'temporary fiscal engine' to make up the shortfall in state revenues. From this point onwards, budget debates in England came increasingly to resemble our own in their arguments over deficits and income taxes. However, the income tax revenues remained less than those from indirect (sales and property) taxes until World War I. Until then, the market, and not the state, was generally understood as the best guarantee of prosperity linked to freedom.

Less is More

This British example is instructive because it shows how political change that *reduces* the power of the state can nevertheless *add* to its policy capacity. To us, a century or more later, it simply looks like constructive evolution in a period of enormous change. Just as Britain struggled to reconcile monarchy and markets, so our struggle is between the legitimacy of public territorial organization and the legitimacy of the private global flows our prosperity is based upon. Monarchy was needed to ensure the continuity and identity of the state. Markets were needed to ensure prosperity with freedom. A middle-class government responsible to a freely voting electorate was the compromise: 'nation' was the term used to seal the bargain.

The way contemporaries told it, the triumph of the middle-class state in England was always contrasted to the supposed dark age of feudalism and royal tyranny. Whereas feudal power was arbitrary, the 19th century British state recognized human rights—although not enshrined in a written constitution, the better to enable those rights to evolve. The issue of making government responsible to Parliament had been worked out centuries before; the thrust of reform was to make Parliament more representative of the new industrial classes.

The result made a middle-class conquest of Parliament the equivalent to control of the state. Parliamentary democracy was strengthened. Even more interesting, the state backed away from *legislating* the operation of the main instruments that made the state and society possible—the market and freedom of the seas. Instead, state revenues were raised domestically and the government spent them in order to uphold free markets and open seas. (From time to time the state intervened to try to make markets work more efficiently and even to reserve certain spheres (such as the family) as separate from market operation.)

If we leap ahead from the issues of reform in the mid-19th century to our own time, we see that we are in a similar period of transformation. Just as in the 19th century the freedoms of a pro-market state offered exceptional opportunity for citizens prepared to take advantage of them, the same is true today. A state that promotes the forming of wired communities also adds to the opportunities of its citizens. If we compare some of the key concepts of governing in the industrial state to those of the wired community, we can derive a table such as the one below.

Individual capacity for action is the underlying difference highlighted by the two columns. The wired community takes the passive concepts of industrial society and adds enormously to what people can do to control their lives and help determine the future directions of the communities in which they have an interest. The Net empowers people to organize and make their views known as well as to undertake actions that have significant consequences. The many Web sites devoted to political activity, together with listservs and discussion groups, are ample testimony to this development. Allied with that is the power of those with IT expertise to build software machines that nullify laws they regard as foolish and without merit.

Table 9.1   State-based Concepts and their Wired Community Extensions

Industrial State	Wired Community adds
Individual rights	Individual empowerment
Legal authority	Nodes, aggregators and code writers
Separation of powers	Loyalty, voice or exit, self-enforcing bargains
Equality before the law	Access, reciprocity and giving (gift culture)
Territory (country) before interest: national sovereignty & independence	Interest transcends (trumps) territory: collective security & interdependence

For example, Pretty Good Cryptography (PGP), a popular encryption program that is freely distributed on the Web, enables ordinary people to achieve a significant level of privacy despite government snooping in some countries. In other cases, the use of anonymous mailers helps safeguard computer use in countries where it is forbidden. Software with all kinds of capabilities circulates freely on the Internet, as does information about hidden features of some off-the-shelf programs. The ability of software coders to offset or nullify legislative coding (national laws) is seen by many as illegitimate, an affront to the democratic process—in some cases just a tad less menacing than outright computer hacking. Yet as we've argued earlier, the process of norming in the digital world depends to a large extent on how *networks*, not legislators, behave. If some activity exhibits appeal despite legislation, the chances are it will simply port to the Net.

Some commentators have argued that the Net can and will evolve from this libertarian type of entity towards a far more controllable space, transmitting sufficient meta-data (i.e. data about the data being transmitted, such as a code identifying the machine that sent it) along with users' messages to end anonymity. Technically, that may well become possible. But if that is implemented beyond a certain threshold, the full promise of the Net will never be realized. People will limit their use of the network in response to what the programmers permit. Freedom of cyberspace is similar to freedom of the seas—and just as important to the successful development of a global, Net-based civilization as freedom of the seas was to the global industrial civilization led by Great Britain. Without freedom of cyberspace, the Net-based, wired economy and its accompanying civil society could lose its unpredictable dynamism. If subject to more controls than the Net community is comfortable with, that community will evaporate and the Net will become about as interesting as the money machine at the local bank.

On the other hand, innovations—whether of policy or technology—that increase individual political capacity, enhance the transparency of Net coding decisions, extend Net access, and facilitate global flows of ideas, trade and investment will add enormously to the prosperity of whatever countries adopt them. What may appear to be a decline of national sovereignty is actually an increase in policy capacity because it expands the *political* capacity to include the new civil society. Once again, less is more.

At the present time, few countries understand this. The United States has done the most to foster the Net and enjoys the lion's share of traffic (most frequently visited Web sites, leadership in e-commerce, etc.) Can the newly wealthy US cyberians lead a reform similar in scope to that of the 19th century English industrial reformers? In the first year of the 21st century, it's far from clear. But there are some indicators.

- The US Net-led productivity increase, if sustained, may well enable governments to meet their contractual obligations to the baby boom generation without cracking.

- US tax structure has already changed so that most taxpayers now pay a higher dedicated social security tax than they do income tax. (But the state still remains dependent on the income tax paid by the top 20 per cent of earners).

- The US income tax rate is the world's lowest. As more and more activity ports to the Web, chances are the US income tax base of high-income earners will expand while other countries that change more slowly may find their bases eroding.

If present trends continue, the US may well become the hub of a global cyber-civilization that is the electronic equivalent of the Victorian Empire of the mid to late 19th century. If other countries—especially Europe—successfully match US results, the Net-based civilization could extend itself more evenly over most of the planet. Indeed, the success of the US in adapting to cyberspace adds to other pressures (like demography) to reinvent the system. Falling costs in the US, together with the weakening tax capacity of the state, should induce substantial change throughout the

developed world. The gradual acceptance of a freedom of the seas principle or doctrine for the Internet could be one result.

Freedom of the Seas and Freedom of the Net?

The old freedom of the seas concept simply meant that governments
would not impose rules on the water: they continued to try to regulate the
behavior of their own citizens and subjects through the nationality of
shipping, according to their countries of registry. Without explicitly
acknowledging the comparison, when governments wish to control
behavior on the Net, they now regulate the ISPs within their own territories, and if possible outside their territories as well. The problem is that
this may or may not stop the targeted behavior. The Net provides individual empowerment such that individuals with the necessary motivation can
find ways around the rules moving operations to more tolerant jurisdictions. The scope of one's capability to do this is established by the architecture of the Net itself. However, the technical side only makes the
transaction possible: there must also be other people willing to do the
same thing in cooperation. In other words, there must also be loyalty and
self-enforcing bargains enabling the (illicit) activity. The problem with
regulating Net activity really arises when enough people support an action
to make it viable, irrespective of some governments' opinion.

When such activity resonates with our values, such as free speech, we
applaud the technology's empowerment capability. When we disap-
prove—child pornography is the usual example—we condemn it. Yet as
with the example of Britain in the 19th century, less can be more. One
approach to improve the effectiveness of regulation in such circumstances
would be to allow ISPs to choose a national 'registry' like a ship. They
would then be regulated according to the standards of the 'flag' nation.
This would be consistent with the character of the Net, but would also
allow ISPs and their clientele to self-organize according to their understanding of acceptability.[xlvii]

Using this approach, political capacity and policy capacity would remain aligned: those wishing protection under particular laws would have a wider range of protection to choose from. If opinion were overwhelmingly against a particular action, then practically no ISPs supporting it would find shelter. The result would be stable because it would be based on public support. By abandoning the sovereign right to impose the unimposable, governments would obtain the right to regulate those who wish the protections so afforded.

Re-thinking Government's Role

Redefining government in the light of changes of this magnitude is not just a question of adding technology to an existing portfolio of organizations and processes. Adding technology must accompany a substantial re-think of what government can actually accomplish in this new state of affairs. Moreover, it's important to make these conversations as inclusive as possible. One hundred and sixty years ago, when Britain was undergoing similar changes, a conversation of considerable depth and complexity occurred, spreading to other countries as they began facing the same challenges to their institutions. Some major classics of liberal political and economic theory, among which are Jeremy Bentham's doctrine of utility, David Ricardo's theories of trade and taxation, John Stuart Mill's contributions to economics and government came out of those conversations.

Today, confronted with the challenge of governing in a digital age, John Stuart Mill is still instructive. For Mill, the aim of government is to facilitate not just rising standards of living but also rising standards of civilization. He vigorously opposes using government in ways that induce dependence on government services, yet he also favors an interventionist government whenever it can have positive results in terms of promoting alternatives and possibilities that expand individual choice. For some of his contemporaries, the dilemma of government lay in choosing whether to support Order or Progress. Mill comes down squarely on the side of progress, without advocating anarchy. He argues that limits to representative government are set by public acceptance. He goes further, to divide government intervention into rule-making by authority, which he expects will decline, and rule-making that creates options for individuals. He warns that even this must be constrained to situations in which government power in general is not thereby increased.

What is particularly pertinent in Mill's and other contributions to the 19th century debate about the role of the state is the importance of individual choice. As with representative government, the key to the effective governance of the Net is freedom of individual choice. A market is very much a network: the market as a whole becomes more efficient as it attracts more people and money. The more efficient the market, the more participants it will attract. The Net shares the same properties: the more people who are connected and the more capabilities the Net offers those people, the more rapidly it will grow and become part of people's lives. Because information costs are so much lower on the Net than in physical markets, efficiencies can be that much greater. For example, the interactive properties of the Net allow parts of it to become self-regulating in ways that markets can't easily duplicate. Thus sites that wish to earmark themselves as especially suitable for children, for example, can form associations and set standards enabling search engines to seek them out and verify the safety of their contents.

But there's more to regulation than self-organization. In real life my choices can hurt you and yours can hurt me. We have laws to restrict a person's freedom of action to the point at which those actions may damage another. What about the Net? The issue is not about the aims, but about the means. In physical space, there is a governing authority that defines, identifies and punishes wrongdoers. This is what a criminal justice system does: it criminalizes some behavior and imposes the lawful deployment of force to clean it up. But there's also another branch of law in physical space: civil law, older, more evolutionary, that works on the principle of demonstrated harm, compensation and the right of each claimant to have access to the courts.

Cyberspace is far more amenable to civil law approaches than criminal law. What's more, there's a jury at work every day—the communities of Net users. A cyber-shop that ignores a customer's complaint can be defamed across the Net, and if Net authorities try to shut the complainant down, the story gets even bigger. Reputation management is a key part of Net presence. The more users, the more likely the site is to be above board, and the more vulnerable to alerts that the company has goofed. For example, persistent attacks on Scientology in a discussion group led, despite government efforts, to the Net expanding the range of public comment on Scientology's claims to religious status.[xlviii] More recently, consumer groups across Europe and North America managed to force their way into OECD meetings on Internet commerce and underline a valuable consumer viewpoint that was relatively unacknowledged in discussions up to that point—namely the threat to "fair use" implications over vigorous application of copyright protection to digital products.[xlix]

Moving the Debate to a Higher Level: Netting Out Some Principles

In contrast to the 19th century debate on bringing democracy and monarchy together, our late 20th and 21st century debates have proceeded on the assumption that existing principles of national democratic sovereignty are sufficient to solve the problem of governance in a global economy linked by computers. Unlike the profound and innovative debates at mid-19th century (or even at the end of the World Wars and the beginnings of the welfare state), we have not yet developed an innovative governance framework for our own future that goes beyond the concepts of government in physical space.

The closest we come to such a framework is the 'don't tread on me' spirit of John Perry Barlow's Cyberspace Manifesto. This amounts to a declaration of cyberspace independence from physical space drawn from the US Declaration of Independence.[1] It's a valuable first step, but is insufficient, because its libertarian principles stand in stark contrast to (1) the origins of the Net as a military public works program and (2) the extent of regulation needed to keep cyberspace commerce operating in the thousands of jurisdictions it links—regulations about telecom infrastructure, contract and consumer laws, payment systems, privacy, etc. A more comprehensive approach to Net regulation can be tracked through the relevant OECD papers on e-commerce on the OECD Web site (*www.oecd.org*). These, however, sidestep the issue of government competence to enforce regulations and make no mention of non-commercial activities in cyberspace. (Many listervs dedicated to on-line democracy are promoting this along with electronic distance voting. See *www.e-democracy.org*)

Underlying all these legal matters is one genuinely new principle that has made a significant contribution to our understanding of the diminishing policy capacity of the state. Lawrence Lessig argues that code writers in private companies are undermining state sovereignty when they design software that imposes conditions on users that conflict with national laws. One example is that users' software licenses often impose more restrictive rules on licensees than would the 'fair use' doctrines of U.S. copyright law. Lessig's remedy is to urge the reassertion of state sovereignty through using a system of certificates to zone the Net according to the wishes of governments.[li] The politics of physical space, he believes, is more legitimate than the non-political, commercially driven, code writing of cyberspace. His arguments stand in dramatic contrast to those of his former Harvard colleagues David Post and David Johnson. Post[lii] argues that governments and Nets have morally equivalent rule sets, except that those of the Net are much easier to move among. Therefore, freedom of movement will exercise its own countervailing power, both on the rules of physical space and on Net-group rules that users dislike.

Both Lessig's and Post's arguments underline the importance of finding a formula to cover the convergence of national sovereignty and a global Internet. Ironically, in view of his position in favor of the state, Lessig suggests that the principle should be *an architecture of confidence* on the Net—confidence that important values will be respected, users will not be harmed and the Net's promise of opportunity and achievement can be fulfilled. This can (and in all probability will) be achieved through the power of individual choice as the natural selector in an evolutionary process. Nations can achieve widespread compliance with commonly accepted standards on the Net by recognizing the limits of their political and policy competence in the area. Less will be more.

If the Net fails to satisfy its publics, they will stop using it and it will cease to grow. A good way to encourage the Net is therefore to legislate it as though it were the ocean—let freedom of the seas prevail. The ships—the Internet Service Providers—will choose their flag for regulatory purposes, and people will pick and choose their ISPs. The users will control the evolution of the Net according to their needs.

What about disputes? There are various commercial mechanisms already available (such as the consumer redress mechanisms now embedded in Visa, MasterCard and others). But we can expect to see the emergence of Netspace courts on the pattern of admiralty courts to handle issues that normal Net-based mechanisms cannot. As confidence in such a system emerges, it will encourage even greater use of the Net. But if confidence wanes, then Net activity will diminish. After a time, we might expect to hear calls for a different regulatory formula, one that turned matters back to states. That, in an optimistic scenario, would increase counter-pressure for more effective Net self-regulation.

An example of this process is taking place now in respect to privacy issues. Europe believes that there are certain rights to privacy that impose upon governments the need for diligence in ensuring that their citizens are duly protected. The US believes that the public duty goes no farther than insisting upon effective self-regulation by those private entities that collect information for commercial purposes. The EU, unsatisfied by this response, threatened in 1999 to impede commerce with the US that imperiled its concept of EU privacy rights. A compromise has been reached (the US will certify certain private sector 'safe harbors' as meeting the European standards), but at time of writing (autumn 2000), the jury is still out on whether the safe-harbor compromise will hold. Failure will further discourage the growth of the Net in Europe as people fear for the misuse of their personal or corporate data.[liii] Meanwhile, private certification-based services are emerging to win consumer confidence. (For example, PrivaSeek, (www.privaseek.com.))

One element behind the more open (i.e. less restrictive for companies) US position is the huge business in consumer databases collected by industries in the US. These are themselves commercial items that companies mine in search of new insights into consumer behavior. The databases themselves have provoked an elaboration of copyright law to fine tune which databases can be protected from unfair use by third parties and which cannot. The details should not obscure the main point: Internet links are forcing governments to articulate their differences in order to meet expectations that may be profoundly different from a pre-Internet world. The safe harbor agreements on privacy provide an example of how many alternative approaches can co-exist on the Net. The ultimate test will be user acceptance or rejection.

The debates of the last century proposed rules in which outcomes would be clear and stable: representative democracy should be thoroughgoing, governments should facilitate citizens' freedom of choice, and the sum would lead to an advancement of civilization. States were thus self-ruling entities pursuing progress in ways that respected and enhanced individual rights. Today's cyberspace/physical space convergence debate provides no such firm principles. One reason is that, unlike a 19th century factory-style organization, cyberspace can't be legislated—not even by its code-writers.

Factory machinery in the industrial era didn't just evolve by itself. *The Internet does.* The Net is a dynamic system that reacts and adjusts to every new element that arrives and every old element that persists or exits. From this point of view, a commitment to individual choice and light regulation amounts to a commitment to allow evolution, guided by changing user preferences, to decide the system's future. Moreover, that evolution can be amazingly rapid, through such processes as increasing returns and 'swarming' as the Infocosm swoops in to praise or condemn.

Yet is not such a system simply a recipe for an endless cycling between such alternatives as more/less state interference; gift culture/commercial culture activity; more/less Internet activity? If so, such cycling will discourage growth unless counterbalanced in some way. The counter-balancing factor has to be phase-change—that is, with each twist of the wheel, the Net must become a better, more congenial place than before. The ability of taxpayers to allocate value to jurisdictions according to perceived value can encourage this. Without being Utopian, it is foreseeable that competition among jurisdictions based on taxpayer value received, will prove to be a positive force.[liv]

The ability of those who use the Net to organize their fiscal affairs will become more important as countries move their affairs increasingly to cyberspace. Governments that set up rules that make cyber activity intolerably restrictive will simply lose revenue to those who take the opposite course. Users will control the system and thereby impart a progressive direction upon it.

The shift to cyberspace will become generally welfare enhancing. The balancing of property rights and explosion of collectively generated wealth will add to prosperity. The new prosperity will add to the capacity of civil society. The new organizational capacity of civil society will ensure a new level of accountability in the world and, ultimately, effectiveness in replacing negative social processes with more positive ones. While this process is not inevitable, it is coherent. What's more, it appears to us, anyway, as the only coherent process available.

#

Chapter 10

The Net Result

"There is no security on this earth. Only opportunity."
—Old Chinese saying

The impact of the new technology propelling us forward lies not in its novelty but in the depth and breadth of its penetration into the way we live. Although most commentary treats computerization as a technological change, in fact the basic technologies have been around a generation or more. What's new is that now just about everyone with access to a computer keyboard has many of the same global capabilities that a multinational company had uniquely only a few years ago. Moving to an information society, we've argued, should be seen as a social revolution more than a technological one. As such, it constitutes an historical break between eras and obliges us to think in new ways about government. Information technology disconnects the economy from territory, disintermediates government from program design and delivery, undermines some of our most cherished policy rationales, and challenges the ability of government to make people pay taxes they don't want to pay. Such sweeping transformations are too big to 'manage'—at least they've proven to be in the past with one major exception, that of mid-19th century Britain.

Now it's up to us to make a change similar in scope and scale and do so successfully to avoid economic dislocation as welfare state debts come due.

Why won't the trends we've discussed simply project the welfare state globally? Close examination makes clear why that is unlikely to happen. The post war state was based on an idea of government that linked citizenship (personal sovereignty) with territory and national law. But a global information economy breaks the link between personal sovereignty and territory. A logged-on professional can for all practical purposes work wherever he can find someone else on-line to hire him. The bargain they strike reflects the global reach of both parties. They will respect national laws—but in ways that arbitrage between their differences, each to their own advantage. De-territorialization of sovereignty is a major change in the powers of the state.

It's not just that territory doesn't matter any more. The new, global state has achieved its global character and prosperity because money is free to move around the world. Open capital flows and the creation of a global capital market that now trades trillions of dollars a day are essential to maintaining the economic stability of the global economy. But their effects on the levers of national economic policy are devastating. No longer can national governments hope to 'beat the market' through policy interventions. For whatever policy any government adopts, the market collectivity can counteract. The only way governments can ensure that national economic performance is optimal is to commit themselves individually to maintaining steady prices. This new reality weakens not just national governments but trade unions as well. For whatever they may seek to gain in the bargaining process will be offset by loss of purchasing power unless it is justified by productivity increases.

Additionally, the new technologies undermine the policy capacity of the welfare state. The welfare state operates on long out of date assumptions about information. It assumes that only *it* collects the necessary information, that *it* analyzes that information more accurately and comprehensively than any other actors in the system and that the fundamental role of the state is to use that information to break down market failures with a supply of government programs. Governments still have an advantage in collecting some kinds of statistical data. And they perform a useful service in analyzing it, especially macro-level economic data. But the existence of the Internet means that government no longer has a monopoly on good analysis or even on a lot of important data. Indeed, this provides a ready example of a how a change in the cost of information forces governments to shift policy direction. Since the adoption of the World Wide Web ten years ago, the focus of public concern has already shifted from data availability to data misuse—by both governments and businesses as well as organized crime.

A further consequence of ubiquitous information is that governments can no longer develop policy on their own—they must reach out through consultation to civil society to achieve agreement on the models. They can't deliver programs alone, either. Government programs can't be effective if they don't match the needs of recipients. 'One size fits all' solutions can no longer be effective. However, matching programs to needs requires the involvement of the target groups. If the designers of the programs are the ones who get the programs, the obvious question is, "What is government's value-added in this chain of events?" Acting as an independent auditor of performance claims of civil organizations is a plausible function for government. But government can't be judge while it is also responsible for spending money on programs.

Besides the technological and economic challenges the global information economy poses to their post-war role, the welfare state faces another, more urgent and far less abstract threat: demographics. Simply put, if governments were private corporations, they'd have to claim bankruptcy protection and go into receivership—unless they could convince their creditors that the productivity growth achieved over the last 10 years will continue over the next 10 to 15 years. Otherwise, their contracted pay-outs exceed by any measure their capacity to pay them. The 'un-funded liabilities' of the pension funds, the medicare programs, and all the other benefits from day care to education to national defense cannot be met on the revenue base governments now enjoy without those productivity increases. The current revenue base is shrinking as the Baby Boomer population ages. Where there are 3-4 workers today for every retired person, within 15 years there will only be two. The new economy's productivity gains are a must to prevent a melt-down in capital markets a generation from now.

Right now, some policy wonks seeking ways to 'fix' or 'reform' the welfare state are eyeing the pool of capital socked away in retirement plans. The question is, can governments ethically tax away the private savings of those who have made a conscious choice to save for the benefit of those who have not saved? Or put another way, will people continue to accumulate if they believe that will occur? Besides, government policy that seeks to tax away private savings can materialize only if the retiring generation allows it—and they have the means to prevent it through clever use of international tax provisions—provisions that are themselves essential for the continued operation (never mind prosperity) of the global economy. One of the biggest changes in the role of the state as a result of the global information economy is that it now no longer has an infinite power to tax. Only increasing productivity will pull the advanced economies through—and this can only be achieved if national governments embrace change enthusiastically, even if it means a much reconfigured and reduced role for themselves.

Effective Government

These reflections raise the question of what 'effective government' means in an information economy. Currently governments are judged on macroeconomic management (debts, deficits, inflation and unemployment) as well as social conditions (respect for human rights, public health performance, rates of poverty, crime, education system performance, and so on).

Should the same standards of effectiveness retain their hold in an information society? If they do, the key to achieving effectiveness will be how well government is able to encourage and involve civil society in linking economic and social conditions. For the first time, the state will come face to face with a stark new challenge: revenue raising will be *directly* linked to public willingness to pay for outcomes—at the point of payment, not just in an election some more or less long time later.

One important change this suggests is that states will begin competing for tax dollars on the basis of their ability to create civic value. The US does an outstanding job of promoting popular capitalism. If I want to keep popular capitalism alive and well, then I'd better pay some taxes in the US. Denmark achieves remarkable success with some of its social programs. If I want to ensure that there are models of effective social programs, then I should look at making some tax contribution perhaps to Denmark. Now I might ask, how do my own community's programs stack up in the areas that matter to me? What civic value does my country espouse and support effectively? Perhaps there will emerge a class of tax brokers who will ensure that your tax payments flow to programs you wish to support, based on civic values and results obtained. This line of reasoning suggests that public sector revenue raising in an information society will have a lot in common with brand management. Government and its programs will have to stand for something and achieve consistent results if they want to ensure a flow of revenue. One key to government success will be its ability to cultivate and maintain taxpayer loyalty.

Another acid test will be how well governments can enlist the active support of civil society in improving social indicators. The mix of public and private sector involvement will vary with local preferences and circumstances. In some cases, governments will act as convenors or single payers, and the private sector will supply or enable the services, drawing inputs from anywhere in the global economy. In some cases, the private sector will design an intelligent device to meet public policy objectives. Its use

may or may not be compulsory, just like V-chips are voluntary but cat-
alytic converters to reduce auto emissions are compulsory. Or, if a sustainable number of citizens wish to pay governments to bring forward
programs—such as medical health insurance—then governments will
supply them directly on terms negotiated with civil society. Governments
will also become more financially innovative, designing programs that
appeal to capital markets and public private co-funding arrangements.
Many jurisdictions will be able to raise money directly for programs
through specially denominated instruments, such as anti-poverty bonds or
education CDs, if they choose to fund such programs. This approach is
actually less novel than it may sound, especially to those who remember
war bonds. Through such methods, what governments lose through the
increased mobility of the tax base, they may recover from investors.

Yet another test of effectiveness will be the extent to which other governments adopt similar methods. One point is clear: the main test of government effectiveness will be how well governments can enlist the active
support of civil society in improving social indicators.

The idea that people will pay taxes on a more voluntary basis is worrisome
to those who believe that government fiscal coercion is necessary to
enhance the general welfare. But this view ignores the reality of the political process now at work in the welfare state. Taxation is a legitimate part of
the social contract if a person can participate in deciding how she should
be taxed. But modern private interest groups who help politicians meet
the expense of winning elections have managed to appropriate a good deal
of that power to themselves on behalf of their members.

One result of that has been a steep decline in the effective oversight of
government. There was no effective check on the expansion of the welfare
state until open capital markets— not legislatures—began to draw the
line in the mid 1980s. And there is no check on civil society, except in so
far as donors can withhold money if they feel the value they want isn't
there. The new economy and the new technologies greatly strengthen the

taxpayer in this particular arms race. That is to be applauded, not regretted. In so doing, it should also strengthen legislatures. Small wonder that as information costs drop, voters want their political representatives to be far more vigilant of the executive branches of government.

There's another advantage to having taxpayers willingly pay taxes. Making the supply of services more generally accessible through competition with other governments and private suppliers will help alleviate global shortages, particularly of education. The increasing tradability of educational services is also bound to increase the supply of high quality, widely accessible, distance-learning packages. As the world's people become more and more connected, the scope of courses available will expand. For those who want to advance and who have the intellectual ability to do so, the increasing shift to the Net will bring with it an end to geographic barriers to educational access. The cliché about 'thinking globally' and 'acting locally', already a private sector reality, will become a reality in the context of government-supplied services, too. The increased use of the Net in matching supply and demand will also trigger a new kind of 'open-source' phenomenon in which users work together to develop the service or product they want.

Enhanced Citizenship

Underpinning our understanding of how the shift to an information society is transforming our ideas of government and social policy is equally a new understanding of citizenship. If new technology empowers people it also thereby confers upon them a new responsibility for using that power. Underlining that responsibility is the importance the Net confers on 'The Gift Culture', that is, the enhanced supply of high quality products and services available through the donation of others. As some economists have recognized, there are classes of goods for which the Gift Culture outperforms in quantity and quality transactional exchanges. A non-tainted blood supply, genuine emotional bonds, certain types of individual attainment, low-cost robust, high performance software are provided to a superior level for reasons other than money, mostly having to do with obligation and status within community. The Net itself became a killer application propelled by such motives (most Net application technology is still free). Citizenship implies obligation that goes beyond transactions. Here, too, the Net breaks new ground.

The Gift Culture and civil society will involve people more directly in the provision of what today are mainly government-supplied services. These activities can be supplied internationally, but must be delivered locally. From this perspective, the focus or power of citizenship will no longer be an abstract connection with a more or less distant state. Rather, it will be the community, the one which people take the time to lend a hand to constructing and maintaining. Because of the reach of the new civil society, much of this activity may also be done by people from one part of the world helping relieve stress in another, like Doctors Without Borders and other relief organizations do now. There's no reason to assume that borders exist around the concept of community any more than they do around countries.

Just as the Net and globalization detach economies from countries, so too they allow people to choose communities irrespective of formal citizenship. The prospect of a territorially rootless citizenship is new. It's a development for which current legal and political arrangements have left little opening. Does the new economy bring territory-bound citizenship to an end? In effect, the Net and the Gift Culture re-purpose politics away from the private towards the accomplishment of public aims—globally as well as locally.

Re-Norming

The Net, the global news networks and the proliferation of linked global NGOs world wide are also interacting to set newer, higher standards of public policy —new standards or norms in public life. Public policy, like consumer goods, is becoming subject to 'net effects'. For network products, accelerating customer acceptance automatically means that the product becomes the industry norm. People begin using it because others are using it. Now networks also promote the adoption of new standards or norms in public life. Public behavior can have the same infectious quality as, say Netscape or Windows, such that it catches on and triggers an avalanche of imitators. In other words, the Net and the Infoscosm have now become a powerful force for public sector re-norming. Savage political rule bordering on genocide can now trigger worldwide response very quickly— strong enough response to lead to war or consumer boycott or both. We saw this in Kosovo, if not in Rwanda. We saw it in a widespread consumer condemnation of some multinational companies for alleged labor practices in developing countries. Increasingly, no place is too remote for video and the Net. As digital video costs plummet, the trend will accelerate. The power of the Net as a political organizing tool and as a consciousness-raiser is already probably without equal in history. The Net and the broader Infocosm can make it more difficult for those who try to sidestep international good behavior guides, such as the Universal Declaration of human rights, etc. The new, wired world is also becoming a global polity, capable of focusing massive attention upon those selected as targets. This is an embryonic process, but already it is changing the meaning of 'acceptable' global conduct by the rich and powerful.

Strengthening the Edges

Our view of the future sees a role for public policy and an evolving but continuing role for governments of different levels. It does not foresee a world government. While there may be a case for having a world body to speak for global issues, the Net actually promotes something quite different and a lot more effective. Rather than concentrating intelligence at the center, and calling on the center to make big decisions, the new system strengthens the edges. Indeed, this is both its strength and its functional advantage. Rather than centralizing intelligence in the system, the Net allows that intelligence to diffuse outward to the individual network user, and enables her to make lots of little decisions. Instead of collecting things in the center, the Net brings it all together at the edges of the system. It allows a level of flexibility and localization that practically eliminates the need for a 'best possible outcome'. It's possible, depending on the local choices made, that the system's flexibility may increase instability. But this is a vigilant system. With eyes, ears and streaming video everywhere, the new system will simply swamp potential miscreants in oceans of protest.

In this sense, the Net becomes a new tool that allows the planet to govern itself through people meeting their needs in flexible ways primarily designed to work locally, but with a strong, painful stinger in the event of transgression. The planet becomes more like a city with a lot of neighborhoods—and interventions always come with an enormous media contingent.

Yes, But...

The Net based economy will do well if it can equal or surpass the progress marked by the welfare state. The industrial welfare state achieved unprecedented levels of prosperity, supported by a framework of humane institutions. These range from publicly supplied education, including subsidies to universities, to income maintenance plans, to publicly supplied health care. The welfare state was the triumph of the World War II generation who wanted a more 'humane' government than the ones that brought on Depression and war. During the period of the postwar welfare state, from 1950 to 1985, North America, Western Europe and Japan in particular, reached their highest levels of prosperity and democracy. That same massive economic success also laid the foundations for the globalized, information-based economy that is replacing that post war state. .

As the Net-based economy continues to deepen its hold on the planet, we can expect output to continue to increase and innovation to abound. Both will do more for world poverty and the environment than any imaginable government programs. Yet this vision isn't an easy one to realize. It requires the leadership and support of anyone who is willing to help take it forward. It also requires some confidence in new technology and a willingness to apply it to the potential for happiness intrinsic to civilization. It will require bold political leadership to embrace discontinuity and radical change. Britain found it in the 1840s, the US found it in the 1930s. Now, the world must find it somewhere.

We end with a final note of caution.

From time to time in this book we raided history to discuss the turbulent impact of deep social and economic shifts that change the character of the state. Perhaps the greatest flaw in the 'California ideology' is the degree to which it ignores the challenge of managing change on this scale. The first stages of globalization included the destruction of the Soviet Union and so much stress on some weak national currencies that deep economic crisis led to ethnic violence. This could be just the beginning. Civilization is a product of tension between calculated and non-calculated forces within the human character and imagination. This clash between (rational) civilization and (atavistic) culture runs through western history and has remained especially intense since the opening years of the last century before World War I. When allied with popular nationalism (in the guise of fascism and national socialism), the non-calculated forces blew the world apart. In the process they demonstrated a vulnerability that remains embedded in western civilization.

A question lurks beneath our own rapidly evolving technocratic civilization: which of these forces does the new technology represent—is it the rational, calculating, market-oriented, benefit-driven aspect of our civilization? Or do the new technologies' power and the excitement of new capabilities belong to the non-calculating, sensation-exploring, ultimately destructive aspect of western civilization? Arguably, this emerging new information-based world is a mixture of both forces. And because of it, the future holds no guarantees. Instead, as we've said before, it comes without instructions and with lots of assembly required.

#

About the Authors

Guy Stanley and Dian Cohen have been tracking the changing economy for more than two decades. Each has won National Business Writing Awards. Dian has been honored with membership in the Order of Canada.

Ten years ago they joined their efforts to describe the new economy, first with a documentary series *The Global Economy* (CJRT Open College, 1990). They explored the importance of innovation (*No Small Change*, Macmillan Canada, 1993) and the emergence of a networked private economy (*Class Action*, Robert Davies Press, 1993). Dian went on to explore the fiscal plight of the advanced countries, especially Canada, which she wrote up in *The New Retirement: Financial Strategies for Life after Work* (Doubleday, 1999, 2nd ed. 2000). In this book they continue their examination with an in-depth look at how the new technologies change the capacities of public sector institutions.

Guy Stanley is the Director of the International MBA Program at the University of Ottawa. Dian Cohen runs an economic communications consulting company with offices in Quebec, Ontario and British Columbia.

Contact them at www.netresults2002.com

Bibliography

This book is a work of reflection; it makes no claim to comprehensiveness. We did not attempt to compile a complete bibliography. Each chapter's endnotes cite texts and Web sites that have been especially helpful in preparing that chapter. We also questioned the usefulness of attempting an extensive bibliography, as the subject of the future of the nation state in a globalized Infocosm is itself evolving so rapidly. Instead, for those who would like to follow these issues as they develop, here are some sites we have found particularly useful:

For government policy and comparative statistics, try the OECD (*www.oecd.org*) and the IMF (*www.imf.org*). Other information on the challenge facing developing countries is posted regularly on the UNC-TAD Web site (*www.unctad.org*) and the UNDP Web site (*www.undp.org*). For the specifics of trade issues, see the WTO (*www.wto.org*). For another take on development issues, see the World Bank (*www.worldbank.org*); for health care concerns, the World Health Organization (*www.who.org*).

Issues of cyberdemocracy can be tracked through Steven Cliff's excellent newsletter and Web site (www.e-democracy.org). For an intergovernment take on emerging civil society, explore the EU Web site (*www.europa.org*) as well as Netaid (*www.netaid.org*) and others mentioned in the text.

Issues of cyberlaw are also tracked on a number of Web sites. A good comprehensive source can be found at The Berkman Center for Internet Law and Society, Harvard Law School (*http://cyber.law.harvard.edu*). For information about the Internet in general, apart from specialized magazines (each of which has its own Web site) like Wired (www.wired.com) there is cyberatlas (*http://cyberatlas.internet.com*) part of the Business and

Internet Technology Network (*www.internet.com*). For essential background, an indispensable source is The Internet Society (*www.isoc.org*)

Finally, for those who like books, a short bibliography of recent pertinent works:

Axelrod, Robert, *The Complexity of Cooperation: Agent-Based Models of Competition and Collaboration*, Princeton Studies in Complexity, Princeton University Press, 1997.

Bartleson, Jens, *A Genealogy of Sovereignty*, Cambridge Studies in International Relations No. 39, Cambridge University Press, 1995.

Breton, Albert, *Competitive Governments: An Economic Theory of Politics and Public Finance*, Cambridge University Press, 1998.

Castells, Manuel, *The Information Age: Economy, Society and Culture*, 3 vols, Blackwells, London, 1998.

Courchene, Thomas, ed., *Policy Frameworks for a Knowledge Economy*, (B4 in the Bell Canada Papers Series) 1998, and

Courchene, Thomas, ed., *The Nation State in a Global/Information Era: Policy Challenges*. Both from McGill Queen's University Press for the John Deutsch Institute, 1997.

Franklin, Jane ed., *The Politics of Risk Society*, Institute for Public Policy Research and Polity Press, Blackwells, Oxford, 1998.

Grossman, Wendy, *net.wars*, New York University Press, 1997.

Hoffman, John, *Sovereignty*, Concepts of Social Thought, University of Minnesota Press, 1998.

Lessig, Lawrence, *Code and Other Laws of Cyberspace*, Basic Books, 1999.

Loader, Brian D., *The Governance of Cyberspace: Politics, Technology and Global Restructuring*, Routledge, London and New York, 1997.

McKnight, Lee W. and Joseph P. Bailey, eds., Internet Economics, MIT Press, 1997.

Pacquet, Gilles, *Governance Through Social Learning*, University of Ottawa Press, 1999.

Richards, John, *Retooling the Welfare State: What's Right, What's Wrong, What Needs to Be Done*, C. D. Howe Institute Policy Study 31, 1997.

Schuler, Douglas, *New Community Networks: Wired for Change*, Addison-Welsley, 1996

Shapiro, Carl and Hal R. Varian, *Information Rules: A Strategic Guide to the Network Economy*, Harvard Business School Press, 1999.

Slevin, James, *The Internet and Society*, Polity Press, Blackwells, 2000.

#

Index

Endnotes

[i] J. Bradford DeLong, *The Shape of Twentieth Century Economic History*, National Bureau of Economic History Working Paper 7569, February, 2000.

[ii] First sustained powered flight, 1903; Bell's telephone, 1876; TV is based on technology patented in 1929. Broadcasting became technically feasible by 1931. The first digital computer was constructed between 1939 and 1942 at Harvard. ENIAC, its successor, was developed in 1946. The first PC was the Apple II, 1977. The Internet, or network of networks based on a common addressing system and communications protocol (TCP/IP, transmission control protocol/Internet protocol) was created in 1983. (Source: Encyclopedia Britannica [www.Britannica.com]).

[iii] Adam M. Brandenburger and Barry J. Nalebuff, *Co-opetition*, Currency Doubleday, 1996; James F. Moore, *The Death of Competition: Leadership & Strategy in the age of Business Ecosystems*, Harper Business, 1996. On the general issue of the pervasiveness of the IT revolution, Robert Gordon, Northwestern University, has launched a debate about the economic impact of the new economy. Citing an impressive amount of statistical evidence, he argues that the new economy is limited to the information technology sector. In particular, even in the US economy, where IT spending has been highest, multi-factor productivity growth in the years 1972-95 has failed to match the rate of the second industrial revolution from 1870-1913. Two points on this in relation to the argument in this book. The Internet only became a mass medium with the advent of the World Wide Web, which has taken off only in the last two or three years of the period Gordon is reviewing. Dramatic as is the impact of the WWW, its e-commerce impact would probably not show up in the range of years that Gordon cites. More importantly, Gordon does not mark a break in economic management between 1913-1972 where, we argue, the developed

world moved from laissez-faire through the Great Depression to the welfare state, only to see those arrangements challenged in the late 1980s by the combination of globalization and the Internet. Our argument is that this challenge will take government back to a system much closer to the setup in 1913 than people raised in the welfare state are used to. Not that governments will give way quietly; rather, we are saying the Net will oblige governments to change. As they do so, we may expect the tax and regulatory barriers to innovation erected since 1913 to fall away, permitting the productivity gains of that 'golden period' (as it is known to economic historians) to be achieved in our own day. Indeed, we argue, that if this does not happen, then contemporary states face financial collapse because of their aging work force. Robert J. Gordon (1999), "Has the 'New Economy' Rendered the Productivity Slowdown Obsolete?" Paper presented at the CBO Panel of Economic Advisors, 2 June.

http://faculty-web.at.nwu.edu/economics/gordon/researchhome.html.
"Does the 'New Economy' Measure Up To The Great Inventions of the Past," National Bureau of Economic Research Working Paper 7833,August 2000, http://papers.nber.org/papers/W7833. Also, "Case Against IT Miracle," Goldman Sachs, Global Economics Weekly, 19 July 2000.

[iv] They do so with tax treaties designed to avoid taxing the same revenue twice—so-called double taxation.

[v] OECD, IMF.

[vi] Industry Canada, Research Publication No. 1, *Global Trends: 1980-2015 and Beyond*, (November 1998), p.11.

[vii] That is, low tariffs and for established shippers, custom pre-clearances—no unforeseen hitches at borders to slow the flow, with audits rather than arbitrary inspections to validate documentation.

viii The history is available in outline form at various places on the World Wide Web (*www.isoc.org*) and in some useful historical accounts in books (notably, Janet Abbate, *Inventing the Internet*, MIT Press, 1999).

ix Brent R. Moulton, *GDP and the Digital Economy: Keeping Up With the Changes*, Bureau of Economic Analysis, May 1999.

x Danny T. Quah, *The Weightless Economy in Economic Development*, CEP and Economics Department, LSE, December 1998.

xi See the UN Web site at *www.uia.org*.

xii For an in-depth account, see Maxwell A. Cameron, "Civil Society and the Ottawa Process: Lessons from the Movement to Ban Anti-Personnel Mines," *Canadian Foreign Policy*, Vol. 7, No. 1(Fall 1999).

xiii *www.wtowatch.org*

xiv Instructive are the low costs of the protest. *Business Week* reported soon after (March 20, 2000) that the cost of bringing together a 60,000-strong coalition of farmers, environmentalists, human and civil rights groups, consumer groups, religious groups, think-tanks and street theatre activists was a mere $200,000. Only five staffers were paid, and some 2,400 participants were able to stay with Seattle families who opened their homes because they supported what the protesters were doing. The WTO and the national negotiating teams who made up the conference are highly paid, full-time professionals whose contracts entitle them to big per diems and comfortable rooms in top-notch hotels. Forget the Establishment ever being cost-effective in relation to protesters. The new civil society can transform any event designed for high-powered insiders into a public media event that it can dominate any time it wants to.

xv Notis Lesbessis, John Paterson, *Evolution in Governance: What Lessons for the Commission?* EU Forward Studies Unit, 1997, pp.26-7.

xvi On the importance of flows, Manuel Castells, *The Information Age: Economy, Society and Culture,*

Vol. 1, The Rise of the Network Society, Chapter 6, "The Space of Flows," Blackwell, 1996, New York, pp. 376-428

xvii *www.husita.org*

xviii *www.idealist.com*

xix Daniel Bell, *The End of Ideology*, 1961, p.397

xx The adjustment bias that conferred an onus upon the deficit country rather than both deficit and surplus countries together was the result of a compromise between the position of Keynes (namely that surpluses were as destabilizing as deficits) and that of US Secretary of the Treasury Harry Dexter White, in establishing the IMF. The US feared that otherwise Britain's use of deficit financing for its post-war recovery would drag down the purchasing power of the dollar.

xxi For most countries, a stable farming population, preservation of family farms and the rural character of the nation still are seen as the products of policies that conflict with efficient markets. Around the world, governments established local rules by paying subsidies to farmers, thus encouraging them to plant or not plant, according to the deliberations of the national agriculture departments. In most countries, therefore, food imports were restricted by national agriculture policies and farm exports encouraged by subsidies. The resulting product surpluses and price distortions depressed agricultural commodity prices so that by the end of the 20th century, they were below the cost of production (thereby generating more pressure for farm subsidies to save family farms), yet food became gradually more expensive owing to import restrictions. Mountains of unsold food commodities were donated (dumped) as relief to developing countries, thereby further distorting price incentives for efficient farming in Third World countries and encouraging the population flight to already heavily overcrowded cities. Substantial material on these issues exists on the Net. A good starting place is the briefing on agricultural issues on the WTO website (www.wto.org)

xxii Andrew Shonfield, *Modern Capitalism*, (1965), p.3.

xxiii Barry Eichengreen, *Globalizing Capital: A History of the International Monetary System*, 1996, Princeton, esp. pp.128-135.

xxiv This argument receives extensive treatment in Richard Sennett, *The Corrosion of Character: The Personal Consequences of Work in the New Capitalism*, Norton (1998).

xxv Industry Canada, Demographic Trends in Canada 1996-2006: Implications for the Public and Private Sectors, Paper Number 4, November 1998, pp. 19-22).

xxvi Productivity Trends: A Canada-US Comparison, Center for the Study of Living Standards, January 1999.

xxvii Avery Shenfield and Loretta Nott, "Where Canada Really Stands," *Canadian Financing Quarterly*, CIBC World Markets, July 27, 2000, p.2.

xxviii *Maintaining Prosperity in an Aging Society*, OECD, 1998, especially text box II.1, p.31 and subsequent discussion, pp.31-39. The discussion in this OECD publication and the working papers on which it is based do not explicitly address productivity issues nor the problem of actually collecting the mandated higher payroll contributions foreseen. The productivity issue is important because it affects assumptions about the attainable growth rate. This is one of the key elements in the debate between exogenous and endogenous growth theorists. (See Philippe Aghion and Peter Howitt, *Endogenous Growth Theory*, MIT Press, 1998, Chapter 1, for an introduction.) Increasing productivity that is reflected in higher incomes would make the high contributions more realizable in that they would represent only a small if any rise in the payroll tax rate. A more likely scenario under our assumptions is for private investment to flow to low-tax areas in order to maximize private savings to some extent at the expense of public saving (government surpluses in high tax countries). This would worsen the European and Canadian problem in relation to that of the US. However, that difference would be narrowed if Europeans had similar investment opportunities to those available to North Americans, including favorable tax treatment of employee options—but both of these require substantial programs of reform.

xxix Peter Hooper, "Comparing Manufacturing Output Levels Among the Major Industrial Countries," Chapter 10, especially Fig. 1, p.25.

xxx Hans Gerbach, "International Productivity Comparisons at the Industry Level," especially Table 5, p.10. This article and the previous reference are chapters 10 and 11 respectively in a report of an OECD Expert Workshop on Productivity: International Comparison and Measurement Issues, 2-3 May 1996, available on the OECD website at *www.oecd.org/dsti/sti/stat-ana/prod/measurement.htm*. The papers are available in .pdf format. For a general discussion of productivity, see also Dirk Pilat, "What Drives Productivity Growth," *The OECD Observer*, No. 213, August/September, 1998, also available on the OECD Web site.

xxxi See Dian Cohen, *The New Retirement: Financial Strategies for Life after Work*, Doubleday, 2000.

xxxii "US to battle Net as tax haven," Peter Spiegel in Washington, *The Financial Times*, July 10, 2000.

xxxiii *Failing to Click On Online Consensus, Financial Times*, Feb. 2001; OECD Progresses toward Achieving an International Consensus on the Tax Treatment of E-Commerce, 12.2.01. www.oecd/media/release/wwo/-15a.htm

xxxiv "Cybercrime," *Businessweek*, February 21, 2000, cover story, p.36.

xxxv Netizens = Citizens of the Net.

xxxvi These comments follow Donald F. Kettl, Reinventing Government: A Fifth Year Report Card, Report CPM1-98, Brookings Institution Center for Public Management, September, 1998. Available on-line at www.brookings.org.

xxxvii See Finn Poschmann and John Richards, "How to Lower Taxes and Improve Social Policy: A Case of Eating Your Cake and Having It Too," C.D. Howe Institute Commentary, February 10, 2000 (Communiqué).

xxxviii The ability of 'bots to search deep into Web pages beyond the opening screen has become a subject of litigation. The issue is followed comprehensively by Profesor Stephan Bechtold, University of Tuebingen, Germany on The Links Controversy Web site *(www.jura-uni-tuebingen.de/~s-bes1/lcp.html)*.

xxxix An inventory of current efforts, as well as a call for participation, can be found at *www.statskontoret.se/*.

xl Karl Polyani, *The Great Transformation:The Political and Economic Origins of our Time*, Beacon Press, 1957. Also, J. Rogers Hollingsworth and Robert Boyer, eds, *Contemporary Capitalism: The Embeddedness of Institutions*, Cambridge University Press, 1997.

xli The U.S. Senate voted 74 to 21 in July 2000 for a proposed amendment that would overturn a 1988 ban prohibiting Americans from re-importing pharmaceuticals that were originally destined for foreign countries. If passed, this would allow American pharmacists and drug wholesalers to buy prescription medications at what would be cut-rate prices from Canadian suppliers.

xlii WHO World Health Report 2000 *(www.who.org)*.

xliii John Acquilla and Donald Ronfeldt, *The Emergence of Noopolitik: Toward an American Information Strategy*, 1999, Rand.

xliv Laura Landon, "Big Brother is watching you," *Ottawa Citizen*, July 22, 2000, D-1.The workplace monitoring report can be found at http://www.amanet.org/research/monit/index.htm.

xlv Charles Tilly, *European Revolutions, 1492–1992*, Blackwell, 1995, p.237.

xlvi The Great Reform Bill of 1832.

xlvii The most permissive national rules would attract the most permissive material. Anyone could still access it, but the activity would become easier to control because, at the margins of tolerance, Web sites would tend to register under 'flags' where tolerance of their most extreme activity was greatest. Countries that were unduly restrictive would see a sharp drop in the number of Web site registrations—as indeed might occur with countries that were unacceptably tolerant. Countries that wished to increase the critical mass of Web sites in their jurisdiction could expand their limits of tolerance up to the point at which customer volume stopped growing.

xlviii Wendy M. Grossman, *net.wars*, NYU Press, 1997, p. 88-89.

xlix See papers on the Consumer Technology Project website, *www.cptech.org*.

l For text and comment, see Grossman, op. cit., pp. 192-194.

li LawrenceLessig, *Code and Other Laws of Cyberspace*, Basic Books, 1999, esp. chapter 14.

lii David Post and David Johnson, Anarchy, State and the Internet: An Essay on Lawmaking in Cyberspace, available online from the *Journal of Online Law*, 1995, as article 3 at *www.law.cornell.edu/jol/post.html*.

liii The safe harbor provisions are designed only to apply to US company treatment of data transfers from the EU. At present, there is no requirement to apply them to US personal data. The arrangement could spur the US to conform more closely to European requirements, although US consumers may be indifferent or will opt for a different, more market-based approach to treatment of personal data. For example, there could be compensation of individuals for data shared with third parties.

[liv] This statement may sound as though it flies in the face of the economic literature on government competition, but it does not. Tiebout competition is stabilizing, in contrast to others. Albert Breton, *Competitive Governments: An Economic Theory of Politics and Public Finance,* Cambridge U.P., 1998, especially chapter 9, p.230.

www.ingramcontent.com/pod-product-compliance
Lightning Source LLC
Chambersburg PA
CBHW051227050326
40689CB00007B/830